MW00928107

Text Copyright © Oliver Cooper

Legal & Disclaimer

The information contained in this book and its contents is not designed to replace or take the place of any form of medical or professional advice; and is not meant to replace the need for independent medical, financial, legal or other professional advice or services, as may be required. The content and information in this book has been provided for educational and entertainment purposes only.

The content and information contained in this book has been compiled from sources deemed reliable, and it is accurate to the best of the Author's knowledge, information and belief. However, the Author cannot guarantee its accuracy and validity and cannot be held liable for any errors and/or omissions. Further, changes are periodically made to this book as and when needed. Where appropriate and/or necessary, you must consult a professional (including but not limited to your doctor, attorney, financial advisor or such other professional advisor) before using any of the suggested remedies, techniques, or information in this book.

Upon using the contents and information contained in this book, you agree to hold harmless the Author from and against any damages, costs, and expenses, including any legal fees potentially resulting from the application of any of the information provided by this book. This disclaimer applies to any loss, damages or injury caused by the use and application, whether directly or indirectly, of any advice or information presented, whether for breach of contract, tort, negligence, personal injury, criminal intent, or under any other cause of action.

You agree to accept all risks of using the information presented inside this book.

You agree that by continuing to read this book, where appropriate and/or necessary, you shall consult a professional (including but not limited to your doctor, attorney, or financial advisor or such other advisor as needed) before using any of the suggested remedies, techniques, or information in this book.

Table of Contents

Introduction

Greetings! It's great that you have finally found time to join us here!

As you know, nowadays a lot of people in our world spend majority of their life on the go. Most of us are overwhelmed with work not only during the week, but on the weekends, as well. This makes us depend on things like fast food. You want to eat healthy, but you just can't afford to spend countless hours cooking? Well, then the Crock Pot might just be the perfect option for you! It saves you a great deal of time, thus helping you to stay on schedule and minimizing the time you spend cooking. Being the owner of the Crock Pot is one thing, but knowing how to maximize the health benefits of using it is another! If you have decided to stick to the Ketogenic diet chances are you have already encountered many challenges. But what if I tell you that the Crock Pot that is standing on the counter in your kitchen is a magic wand you have simply forgotten about? Are you looking for recipe ideas that would be delicious and also follow the rules of the ketogenic diet? In this case, I assure you, my friend, you have found just the right book!

This book is perfect for food-loving Crock Pot owners that follow the ketogenic diet, as it provides a lot of useful information regarding the state-of-the-art capabilities of the Crock Pot and the benefits of the ketogenic diet. The ketogenic diet does include lots of «complicated» rules, but it will be much easier to follow them using this book and the recipes in it. The recipes of the Keto Crock Pot Cook Book are rather simple, accessible, adaptable and easy to understand and to make in the Crock Pot that is already in your kitchen! Now it will be so much easier to enjoy your favorite foods! The recipes in the cookbook are divided into chapters, so that finding them becomes a piece of cake. So, let's cook together and have some fun!

Chapter 1: the Keto Diet & the Crock Pot

What Is the Ketogenic Diet?

A ketogenic or simply a keto diet is a popular modern low-carb diet. It forces the body to use small fuel molecules that are called "ketones" as the main energy source. The liver breaks down fats into fatty acids and ketones, when the blood sugar levels are low. The glucose is actually the easiest molecule in the body to break down and that is why it is usually used as the main energy source. If a person eats food high in carbs, the organism begins to produce both insulin and, of course, glucose. Insulin is generated by the body to bring the glucose into the bloodstream taking it around your body. There is no need for the body to process the fats since the glucose supplies energy. In this case, fats are stored in the body. Lowering the consumption of carbohydrates induces ketosis in the body. The ketones are generated by the body if a person consumes a small amount of carbs that are quickly broken down and a plenty of protein. The ketones produced by the liver are used to fuel important organs, including the brain. The latter needs a lot of fuel to fulfill even the simplest daily functions, but cannot run on fats, only on ketones or glucose. The main aim of a ketogenic diet is to force the body into the metabolic state. The human's body is incredibly adaptable to everything an individual puts into it – as soon as a person overloads the body with fat, taking away all carbohydrates, it quickly begins to process and burn the ketones. The optimal keto level is a great way to stay healthy and lose excess weight, as it has both mental and physical benefits. This book can be your assistant on the journey to the keto-diet world.

What You Can Eat during the Ketogenic Diet

If you are an individual that is not completely sure what is allowed during a keto diet and what must be strictly avoided, this part of our book will be of tremendous help for you! Sticking to any diet isn't easy, I think most women know what I'm talking about. It gets more complicated when you have no idea what you should consume during the day. It may become a real challenge to keep a keto diet if it is new for you. But the recipes, meal plans and shopping lists included in this book will make your keto-life so much easier. Remember the main rule - following this diet you have to be focused on eating real food that is also low in carbs. A short list of allowed products and of those, you must avoid provided below. An easy visual guide of products that fit in with the requirements of a ketogenic diet is amazing for beginners who would like to make the right decisions on what exactly to eat and, of course, shop for.

- ***Oils and fats***

Fats must make up the majority of the calories you consume in a day. Here you have the options to choose from, what you prefer and what you don't like. Basic lovely dressings, sauces and toppings could be added to falafel or soy meat in any combination your heart desires! Fats are significant for the organism, but too many of them could potentially have adverse effects on your body. The ketogenic diets involves the consumption of the following types of fats: saturated (like ghee, butter, green bacon, coconut oil); as well as monounsaturated fats (nut, avocado, olive oil). Be careful with polyunsaturated fats. Trans-fats – try to avoid entirely! This fat has an altered chemical composition and can lead to heart disease. Keep a balance between the levels of omega 6's and omega 3's, consuming lots of tuna, wild salmon, trout will help you to keep the balance necessary for your health. Be careful with the consumption of seeds and nuts as they are a source of omega 3's. Almonds, pine nuts, walnuts, corn oil fall into this category. The food that could be ideal for your keto diet is – avocado, ghee, butter, mayo, macadamia/avocado/olive/coconut oil, cocoa and coconut butter, vitellus, tallow.

- ***Protein***

You shouldn't consume too much protein either, because it can cause the levels of ketone production to decrease, which means your body will have to rely on glucose. Here are some examples of protein you are allowed to consume: eggs; cheeses, soy meat nut butter (unsweetened and natural nuts, try to find the versions that are higher in fats).

- ***Fruit and veggies***

The best vegetables for this diet are green and leafy, as they are grown above the ground. When it comes to veggies that grow below the ground, consume them in moderation. Actually, if there is a vegetable you really love or crave, the rule here is to just consume it in moderation. The vegetables that you are allowed to eat are: spinach, lettuce, chives, radicchio, endive, etc.; radishes, kale, kale turnip, asparagus, summer squash, cucumber, bamboo shoots. When eating berries try to control the levels of carbs in them.

- ***Dairy (milk)products***

Milk products are usually consumed by an individual within a keto diet in a combination with a variety of other variety of products. The most part of foods consumed by an individual must be based on veggies and added fats. Favored are organic, raw products, high in fats. For those individuals who are lactose sensitive, it is important to try and consume pasteurized and hard dairy. The allowed dairy products are: mozzarella, blue, brie, Monterey Jack, Greek yogurt, spreadable, hard cheese (Swiss or etc.), mayo, mascarpone, sour crème etc.

- ***Seeds and nuts***

You may consume seeds and nuts, especially when they are parched, using them as appetizers or as flavorings to the main dish. If possible try to exclude peanuts, as these nuts are legumes. I think, you know, the nuts are a perfect source of fat, that's why when consuming them you must carefully balance the levels of protein you consume. Next time around, you open a pack of nuts, remember what you are allowed to eat: Brazil and macadamia nuts, pecans, almonds, walnuts, pine nuts, peanuts and hazelnuts.

- ***Spices and cooking***

Sauces and seasoning are an intricate part of the keto diet, but the good news is that you can continue to make/use your favorites. There is no reason to list all of the allowed spices, as there is a great number of them. Some of them are amazing to use, however the others – have a high glycemic index. The sea salt is preferable over table salt. The spices that are allowed during this type of a diet are: cinnamon, chili powder, cayenne pepper, Greek oregano, cumin, cilantro, basil, rosemary, parsley, thyme. Be sure, you can consume pepper and salt without worrying.

- ***Sauces and condiments***

The sauces as well as other condiments are at the twilight zone on keto diet. This is due to the fact that if you try to strictly stick to the keto diet, the premade sauces must be avoided altogether, because they may contain the commonly obtained sugars and sweeteners that aren't appropriable on the diet. The sauces or some gravies that you select to cook must be based on xanthan gum or guar. They are much lower in carbs than the others. Also, if you are buying a premade sauce, read the label attentively! The allowed sauces are: mustard, Dijon mustard, ketchup, hot sauce, mayo, sauerkraut (without sugar or low in sugar), relish, Worcestershire Sauce, salad dressings (the fattier ones), flavored syrups (with permitted sweeteners).

- *Sweeteners*

It will be not so easy to keep this keto diet for those individuals who love sweets. But doing this is possible and you do have two options – either keeping your sweets intake on almost a zero level or using the substitutes. If you still wish to consume sweeteners, chose the fluid versions. You may also identify which one tastes better for you as there is a great number of diverse sorts and new altered substitutions of them. The most popular are: Stevia (preferred in liquid form), sucralose (rather sweet substitution), monk fruit, erythritol etc.

- *Beverages*

Among the preferred beverages when sticking to a keto diet are: coffee with coconut milk or cream, water, black or herbal tea.

What you can't eat during the ketogenic diet
And now, when you already have a clear idea about which products you might consume during a

ketogenic diet, it is the time to complete the list of forbidden products. If you still are not sure about the products that aren't keto appropriate, this list of limitations will definitely help you:

- Sugar – it can be found almost in all soda, mostly all juice, the plurality of sports drinks, sweet candies (even if these are your favorite ones!), chocolate, ice cream.
- Grains - the wheat products (these include also bread and buns), gruels, pasta, cakes, paddy and corn, beer must be avoided too. This also includes the whole grains like rye, wheat, buckwheat, barleycorn and quinoa.
- Starch – during the keto diet an individual has to avoid some vegetables (like potatoes, yams) oats, etc. Only some of the vegetables are edible but in moderation.
- Trans-fats – paste-like butter substitutes, like margarine and other variations of it should be avoided as they contain hydrogenated fats. These are also bad for our health.
- Fruit – a person who is sticking to the low-starch diet must avoid consuming large fruits like apples, bananas, oranges, because they are extremely high in sugar. Consume the berries in moderation, check the labels if you buy them at the store.
- Low-fat foods – these products are usually much higher in carbs and sugar than the other full-fat versions. Be sure you read the package at the store to avoid making mistakes.

- Milk isn't recommended for a number of reasons. First of all, it is rather complication to digest; it lacks the "good" bacteria and even contains hormones. Also it is high in starch (containing about 5 grams of starch per 100 ml). As for coffee and tea, if you prefer to drink them with milk, substitute milk with cream, but, like with everything else, in moderate amounts.

- Sweet and alcoholic drinks (sweet wine, beer, all the mixed drinks, etc.).

- Pistachios and cashews - consume rarely as they're very high in starch (for example, two handfuls of cashews contains a daily maximum for starch intake).

Benefits of the ketogenic diet

There is a huge variety of diets that come and go, but the ketogenic or the keto diet having been developed not so long ago is gaining increasing popularity. This type of diet is fully based on your knowing the theory and understanding nutritional science and human physiology. When in most diets an individual relies upon counting the consumed calories, sorting the portions, avoiding fats strictly, the keto diet works in a completely different manner, by changing the «fuel source» that an individual uses to obtain energy and be fit all day long 7/24. But the ketogenic diet wasn't greeted by all scientists with open arms right away. Since 2002 more than 15 studies were conducted based on the rules and principals of the ketogenic diet. Almost everyone has proved that this diet was at the top three of all diets. Next, I will list the advantages of a keto diet, they are 1 – the ketogenic diet kills the appetite: hunger was always the adverse reaction to any diet you have already practiced. This is the main reason why individuals dislike and terminate the diets. Consuming fats and low-carb products reduces the appetite. 2 – Sticking to the keto diet allows you to lose more weight than with other diets: the main reason being that the low-carbs tend to get rid of the excessive liquid stored in the human body. People, who stick to this keto diet can lose weight twice as fast. The keto-diets seem to be effective for up to 5 months, after this time an individual's body begins to push back, it occurs usually when people give up and begin to eat the old way. 3 – Getting rid of the fat in the abdominal area. The bodies of the individuals differ from each other. People have two main fat storage locations – in the abdomen, the visceral fat, and, the subcutaneous fat, stored under the skin. The keto diet reduces the visceral fat of the organism, the increased amounts of which could lead to insulin stamina, distraction, and are the mainspring of metabolic indigestion. 4 – The levels of fat moieties called triglycerides tend to go down to zero. 5 – The level of the high-density lipoprotein (HDL) that is also called the «good» cholesterol could be increased due to the keto diet. The higher is the level of the individual's HDL, the lower is the risk of suffering from heart disease. Eating fat is the best way to increase your HDL level. 6 – The ketogenic diet reduces the insulin levels and the level of blood sugar because an individual avoids consuming the carbs that are dragged down into glucose in the gastrointestinal tract. 7 – The ketogenic diet reduces the high blood pressure and as a result, the risk of saccharine disease gets lower. 8 – It is a good way to fight against the metabolic syndrome. The last one is the medical condition that is also combined with heart problems risk and diabetes. 9 – The keto diet is good for brain disorders because of the therapeutic effect. A part of an individual's brain can incinerate the glucose only. But the others one can also burn ketones that are mostly formed, for example during starvation. The method of the keto diet was applied earlier for treating epilepsy in kids. Nowadays this diet is being used for treating Parkinson's and Alzheimer's disease.

Keto for beginners

Now you know a lot about the ketogenic diet, what to eat and what products are not allowed. I hope you have already understood how healthy this type of diet is and you are going to stick to it, just like I will. Sure, every beginning is rather complicated, but if you have a Crock Pot in the kitchen it solves the majority of problems that could arise. In order to decrease the difficultness of the keto beginning, try to consume keto foods slowly, week after week. Remember that the keto diet could change the mineral and water balance in the body, that's why you may add some extra salt to the consumed foods. It is essential to eat until you feel fool, avoiding restricting calories too much. A short list of frequently asked questions about the keto diet using the Crock Pot will definitely help you at the starting stage:

- Is it dangerous for health to stop eating carbs completely? – No, after some months (2-3) you might eat them occasionally, but then return to the keto diet cooking your meals in the Crock Pot.
- I have heard ketosis is dangerous. Is it true? – Don't mix up the ketoacidos with ketosis. Ketoacidosis occurs in uncontrolled diabetes. By the way, using your Crock Pot for cooking is already much healthier than usual cooking.
- Do I have to count my calories? – Be attentive of them, read the labels at the markets and avoid trans-fats and sweeteners.
- Can I prepare the dishes late in the evening to eat them in the morning for breakfast? – Sure, cook in your great helper (the Crock Pot) and then turn on WARM, in the morning you will have the warm breakfast at the table.
- How much protein should I eat? – Don't eat too much, the high levels of it could increase the insulin level in the body. Consume not more than 30-40% of general calorie intake.
- Is it possible to combine the keto diet with the fast pace of my life as I work all day long 7/24? – Sure! This keto Crock Pot cookbook is definitely for you! Save time, eat well and stick to the diet!

Moreover, the keto diet using the crock pot is great for diabetics, people who are overweight, busy men and women, moms and dads.

Crock Pot. What is it?

I feel like everyone has heard of a Crock Pot at least once in their life. It appeared in 1970 and was marketed as a bean cooker. But as it was modified people started to use it to heat up food and keep it warm for prolonged periods of time. And look how far we've come; people are cooking delicious healthy meals in it. It is a perfect small kitchen appliance that consists of a glass lid, a porcelain or a ceramic pot (it is inside of the heating unit) and, of course, a heating element. The modern Crock Pots could be of an oval or a round shape and of various sizes, from small to large. All the Crock Pots have two settingss: LOW (it corresponds to the temperature of 200°F mostly) and HIGH (up to the temperature of 300°F). The WARMing option that is among the options of the majority of the Crock Pots nowadays allows to keep the prepared dishes warm for a long periods of time. Some of the Crock Pot models have a timer that allows you to control cooking time if you are busy.

What Are the Benefits of Using the Crock Pot?

What is the most difficult thing for you in the kitchen? You spend too much time in the kitchen when you might go to the cinema with friends? You spend too much money for products and your ideas for what to prepare today are running out? I know the solution to all your problems… It is the Crock Pot!

Firstly, it is possible to prepare meals when you are not at home. During those hectic family mornings, just throw all the ingredients together following the recipe, switch the machine on and go work.

Secondly, you don't like washing the dishes? Neither do I! Just clean the Crock Pot and the plates after delicious meals. That's all! Using the Crock Pot means having fewer dishes to wash.

Thirdly, the Crock Pot cooks the delicious meals and saves your money!

These meals taste even better than usual and also you can keep the leftovers in the refrigerator to eat later. How perfect are the spice flavors if you eat the dishes right after cooking! You might taste the cayenne pepper, cumin, ginger and other favorite spices of yours. Buy simple products and follow the cookbook. It is easy!

Fourth benefit, the Crock Pot is the best way to keep your meal tender and always warm.

Fifth, the Crock Pot reduces calories and fat. No oil (just olive or avocado oil), no frying is necessary.

Six, step by step preparation.

Step by step preparation facilitates the everyday cooking especially for those who are not great fans of this process. In most recipes, all the ingredients are added at one time to the Crock Pot.

Seven, it is energy saving. It requires less electricity than the usual oven.

The flexibility of the Crock Pot is benefit number eight. You can take it on a trip, put it on the kitchen table or somewhere else. It doesn't need that much space.

And finally, benefit number nine is in the large quantities of prepared meals. Most of these recipes make large quantities of the end products, so you may feed an entire family and even freeze for tomorrow to make easy and quick lunches or suppers.

So, are you already looking for some recipes to get started? Check my great keto Crock Pot cookbook and you'll find the best and most delicious dishes here! Cooking keto recipes in the Crock Pot will help you to fit cooking into your daily schedule and stay healthy. After a long working day, you'll be back home and a delicious meal will be there waiting for you.

Chapter 2: Breakfast Recipes

Crock Pot Vegetable Soup

This recipe of vegetable soup is excellent for calming the nervous system. You may also add the other herbs according to your own tastes or tastes of your family. Blend the mixture until smooth once the cooking time is over.

Ingredients (11 servings):

Cauliflower	1 head
Watercress	½ cup
olive oil	2 tablespoons
sweet onion	1 medium
leek	1pcs
celery 1 stalk	
water (or vegetable stock) 6 cups	
bay leaf	1 pcs
thyme	1 branch

sea salt	2 pinches
dill	1/4 cup

black pepper at will

Directions:
1. Peel and chop the onion. Set aside.
2. Chop the leek, celery, dill.
3. Chop finely the cauliflower.
4. Take a medium-sized skillet, heat the olive oil over medium heat.
5. Add onion, leeks, celery into the skillet and cauliflower florets. Cook about 5 minutes, the onions must be translucent.
6. Add water thyme, and salt at will, bay leaf to the Crock Pot, pour the ready-made veggies from the skillet.
7. Cover the Crock Pot and set on HIGH for 3 hours.
8. Using a blender blend the soup until smooth mix.
9. Add black pepper or cilantro and serve.
10. Dress with watercress.
11. Bon Appetite!

Crock Pot Broccoli Tofu Soup

This easy Crock Pot recipe is great if you need a healthy meal but you don't have time to prepare this meal. It is quick, healthy, full of minerals and vitamins, keto-friendly and tasty! Add Tofu cheese for garnish or fresh basil leaves!

Ingredients (9 servings):

broccoli florets	5 cups (about 16 ounces)
yellow onion	1 medium
garlic	3 cloves
dried oregano	1 teaspoon
freshly grated nutmeg	1/4 teaspoon
vegetable broth	2 1/2 cups
kosher salt	1/2 teaspoon
black pepper	1/4 teaspoon
Tofu cheese low-carb	1 (8-ounce) block

Directions:
1. Peel the onion and slice finely.
2. Peel the garlic and mince.
3. Chop the broccoli florets.
4. Open the Crock Pot and put the broccoli, onion, and garlic in the bottom of the Crock Pot. Add oregano, nutmeg, and vegetable broth.
5. Add Tofu. Cover the Crock Pot and set on HIGH for 2 hours.
6. Once the cooking time is over, use the blender and puree the soup, it must be of smooth consistency.

7. Serve warm. Season with fresh parsley or grated Tofu.
8. Bon Appetite!

Easy Vegetarian Roasted Chestnut Soup

I know that not everybody likes chestnuts, but if you still like, you will definitely cook this soup recipe! This vegan chestnut soup is delicious and light. I advise you to check the soymilk when you will buy it at the store as some kinds of them contain sugar.

Ingredients (9 servings):

olive oil	3 tablespoon
celery	1 rib
onion	1 pcs
strong vegetable broth	6 cups
fresh parsley	1/4 cup
ground cloves	1/4 teaspoon
bay leaves	2 pcs
chestnuts (roasted and peeled)	12 oz.
unsweetened soymilk	1/4 cup

Salt and pepper at will

Directions:

1. Mince celery. Peel the onion and mince.
2. Wash the parsley and chop.
3. Peel and the cloves and mince finely.
4. Peel and roast the chestnuts.
5. Take a large saucepan, saute minced garlic, celery, onion with oil until softened, about 7 minutes.
6. Open the Crock Pot, add vegetable broth. Add chopped fresh parsley, cloves, bay leaves and the chestnuts. Put the mixture in the skillet. Add soymilk.
7. Toss everything well. Put the Crock Pot on HIGH for 3 hours.
8. Once the cooking time is over, take off the bay leaves, using a blender make a puree.
9. Dress with salt and pepper before serving.
10. Bon Appetite!

Crock Pot Keto Aubergines

An easy vegetarian Crock Pot recipe, full of summer flavors is great for hot sunny days. Simply easy put the ingredients in the morning to the Crock Pot and this one will be ready for dinner, supper or lunch. Enjoy!

Ingredients (14 servings):

olive oil   4 tablespoon

red onion   1 pcs

garlic	2 cloves
aubergines	1 lb
ripe tomatoes	6-7 pcs
fennel bulb	1 small
sundried tomatoes	3-4 pcs
coriander seeds	1 teaspoon

Dressing:

flat leaf parsley	¼ cup
basil	¼ cup
chives	2 teaspoon
olive oil	2 tablespoon
juice of lemon	1 pcs

Topping

toasted flaked almonds	½ cup

keto bread for serving

Directions:
1. Peel the red onion and slice. Peel the garlic and crush it.
2. Slice the bulb.
3. Wash the tomatoes and cut.
4. Wash parsley and chop, wash the basil leaves, chop the chives.

5. Squeeze the juice of a lemon.
6. Open the Crock Pot, pour a little bit olive oil into the Crock Pot, put the onions into the bottom, add crushed garlic.
7. Wash and slice the aubergines into thick slices and salt. Put them into the Crock Pot on top of the mix from onions and tomatoes, fennel and sundried tomatoes.
8. Spread the coriander seeds, season well with salt and pepper.
9. Cover and cook on LOW for 7 hours, the aubergines must be softened.
10. Prepare the dressing – mix together parsley and basil, olive oil, juice of lemon, chives.
11. Transfer the ready dish to a serving plate and drizzle with the dressing.
12. Top with flaked almonds and serve with keto bread.
13. Bon Appetite!

Italian Vegetable Keto Bake

An Italian vegetable dish prepared in the Crock Pot, full with sunny courgettes, tomatoes, herbs, and aubergine is irresistible! You may cook this keto dish for parties as an addition to the main dish or eat it without anything.

Ingredients (7 servings):

garlic	3 cloves
tomato	1 can

bunch oregano	
pinch chili flakes	
baby aubergines	11oz
Courgettes	2 pcs
roasted red peppers	½ large jar
beetomatoes	3 pcs
bunch basil if desired	
green salad at will	

Directions:
1. Peel the garlic and mince.
2. Chop tomatoes from the can
3. Wash the courgettes and slice, chop baby aubergines. Slice tomatoes.
4. Open the Crock Pot, put the garlic, chopped tomatoes, oregano leaves, chili and some seasoning, add olive oil if necessary.
5. Add chopped aubergines, tomatoes, courgettes, red peppers, basil and remaining oregano. Repeat vegetable layer, herb, and tomatoes. Push down well to compress, set on HIGH for 5 hours.
6. Serve with the basil leaves and the green salad.
7. Bon Appetite!

Vegetarian Korma Crock Pot Keto

Today I would like to present you an exotic Indian dish, extremely flavorful and spiced. I usually serve this keto dish with cooked cauliflower rice and keto bread. Enjoy the real Indian food full of tasty veggies and an unreal mix of species.

Ingredients:

vegetable oil	1 1/2 tablespoons
onion	1 small pcs
fresh ginger root	1 teaspoon
garlic	4 cloves
fresh jalapeno pepper	1 pcs
ground unsalted cashews	3 tablespoons
tomato sauce	1 (4 ounces) can
salt	2 teaspoons
curry powder	1 1/2 tablespoons
frozen onions	1 cup
green bell pepper	1/2 pcs
red bell pepper	½ pcs
fresh cilantro for garnish	1 bunch

Directions:
1. Peel the onion and slice.

2. Mince fresh ginger.
3. Take off the seeds from jalapeno pepper.
4. Peel the onion and mince.
5. Chop the previously wash pepper, remove the seeds and chop finely.
6. Take a medium-sized skillet, heat the oil over medium heat. Add the onion, cook until tender. Add ginger and garlic, continue cooking 3 minutes.
7. Open the Crock Pot, add pre-cooked mix, put jalapeno, toasted cashews, tomato sauce. Add frozen onions.
8. Place into the Crock Pot bell peppers, add curry powder, cover and put on LOW for 3 hours.
9. Garnish with cilantro.
10. Enjoy!

Crock Pot Easy Keto Soup

You know, something happens to fresh vegetables usually when they are cooked slowly for a long time in the Crock Pot. Your kitchen is full of aromas and the veggie soup is super tender and light!

Ingredients (5 servings):

Leeks	8 oz (225 g)
spinach	8 oz
onion	1 pcs small
vegetable stock	2½ pints

bay leaves   2 pcs

salt and black pepper at will

fresh chives for garnish

Directions:
1. Trim and wash the leeks, cut into 2-inch pieces.
2. Peel chop finely the onions.
3. Wash and cut the spinach.
4. Open the Crock Pot and put the leeks, onion, bay leaves, dressed with pepper and salt. Add vegetable stock.
5. Cover the lid and put on LOW for 3 hours.
6. When the time is almost finished, open the lid and put spinach.
7. Serve warm fresh chives, dress with pepper and salt.
8. Bon Appetite!

Crock Pot Vegetarian Stew Keto

One of my favorite flavor vegetarian stews is this one. If you want to get the creamy texture of it, use the blender or the food processor you have at home and blend the stew at the end of the cooking.

Ingredients (11 servings):

Onion   1 medium pcs

Celery   1 stalk

Kale	4 cup
garlic	4 clove
Italian Seasoning	1 teaspoon
diced tomatoes	1 can
pumpkin	2 cups canned
sea salt	1/8 teaspoon
black pepper, ground	1/8 teaspoon

Directions:
1. Peel the onions, chop finely.
2. Chop the leek. Chop the kale.
3. Peel the garlic and mince.
4. Open the Crock Pot and put everything into the Crock Pot, cover the lid and set on LOW for 7 hours.
5. Once the time is over, serve the dish tor and season additionally with black pepper.
6. Bon Appetite!

Crock Pot Pumpkin Chili

Have you ever tried pumpkin chili recipe? Not yet!? Poor you! It is amazing, flavor, delicious recipe. Smooth texture and tender veggies are perfect! You may also add other variations of veggies if you don't like tomatoes, onion or something else.

Ingredients (11 servings):

diced tomatoes	2 (14.5-ounce) cans
pumpkin pureed	1 cup
diced yellow onion	2 cups
yellow bell pepper	1 medium pcs
chili powder	1 teaspoon
cinnamon	1 teaspoon
cumin	1 teaspoon
nutmeg	¼ teaspoon
ground cloves	¼ teaspoon
kosher salt	½ teaspoon
ground black pepper	½ teaspoon

Directions:
1. Peel the onion and dice finely.
2. Wash the pepper and slice finely.
3. Open the Crock Pot, put diced tomatoes, pumpkin puree, onion, pepper, a little bit chili powder, cinnamon, cumin, nutmeg, ground cloves, pepper and salt at will.
4. Toss everything together. Add water if needed.
5. Cover the lid and put on LOW for 4 hours.
6. Serve hot!
7. Bon Appetite!

Crock Pot Tomato Soup

Crock Pot tomato soup is perfectly well on hot summer days. Do you know my keto bread recipe? Not yet? Search quickly for this recipe and enjoy with colorful tomato soup during hot days. Serve with fresh parsley, dill or basil leaves.

Ingredients (10 servings):

Diced Tomatoes Canned	56 ounces
Vegetable Broth/Stock	2 cups
yellow onion	½ pcs
dried thyme	1 teaspoon
oregano	1 teaspoon
garlic	½ teaspoon
salt	½ teaspoon
black pepper	¼ teaspoon
Bay Leaf	1 whole
Butter	4 tablespoons

Parsley or dill for garnish

Directions:
1. Peel the onion and cut finely. Peel the garlic and mince it.
2. Open the Crock Pot, put diced tomatoes, vegetable stock, onion, dried thyme, oregano,

minced garlic, salt at will, bay leaf, black pepper, butter. Toss everything well.
3. Cover the lid and put on LOW for 3 hours.
4. Once the cooking time is over, serve the ready-made tomato soup to the deep plates. Eat with keto bread.
5. Bon Appetite!

Crock Pot Spaghetti Squash

This vegan spaghetti squash is the best one among vegan recipes. You may it this with various dressings, vegetables, sauces. To cook spaghetti squash in the Crock Pot is so easy! No efforts, no troubles, you don't need to wash a huge number of dishes! Simplicity is a virtue!

Ingredients (2 servings):

squash	1 pcs large
water	1-2 cups
salt at will	

Directions:
1. Take squash that corresponds to the size of a Crock Pot.
2. Wash it and make some holes with fork Pierce 4-5 times.
3. Put the squash in the Crock Pot, add water.
4. Cover and put on HIGH (4 hours).
5. Take off the squash to a plate, let it cool 25 minutes.

6. Cut the squash in half lengthwise, separate the strands by pulling a fork along the flesh.
7. Bon Appetite!

Crock Pot Mediterranean Eggplant salad

You may eat Mediterranean eggplant salad both hot and cold – anyway it is delicious! I tried two ways of its cooking – roasting the onions with peppers or adding them to the Crock Pot at once. You may also add other species to get the dish more flavor.

Ingredients (6 servings):

red onion	1 pcs large
bell peppers	2 pcs
eggplant	1 large
whole tomatoes	1 24 ounces' can
smoked paprika	1 tablespoon
cumin	2 teaspoons
salt	1 teaspoon
black pepper to taste	
juice lemon	1 pcs

Directions:
1. Peel and slice the onion.

2. Wash, take off the seeds and slice sweet peppers. Set aside.
3. Wash and quarter the eggplant.
4. Squeeze the juice of a lemon into a cup.
5. Open the Crock Pot, add the juice of lemon, pepper, cumin, paprika, onion, tomatoes, eggplant, peppers, salt. Stir everything well.
6. Cover and put on LOW for 6 hours.
7. Enjoy hot with keto bread!
8. Bon Appetite!

Keto Vindaloo Vegetables

This dish is great for those who like one-pot meals. It could be eaten as an addition to the main dish or as a separate dish. You may add here also other veggies you prefer. Don't cook the veggies more than mentioned time, otherwise, your veggies would be mushed.

Ingredients (14 servings):

garlic	3 cloves
ginger	1 tablespoon
ground coriander	1 1/2 teaspoon
ground cumin	1 1/4 teaspoon
dry mustard	1/2 teaspoon
cayenne pepper	1/2 teaspoon
turmeric	1/2 teaspoon

cardamom	1/4 teaspoon
vinegar	1 tablespoon
yellow onion	1 large
cauliflower florets	4 cups
tomato paste	6 ounces (one small can)
zucchini	2 small
bell pepper	1 small

Salt and freshly ground black pepper to taste

Directions:
1. Peel the garlic and mince.
2. Peel the ginger and chop.
3. Peel the onion and chop.
4. Wash and cut zucchini into 1/3-inch pieces.
5. Wash and take off the seeds from the bell pepper, slice.
6. Mix garlic, ginger, coriander, vinegar, cardamom, turmeric, mustard, cayenne pepper in a blender. Mix until smooth. Set aside.
7. Add to the Crock Pot smooth mixture, cauliflower florets, zucchini, peppers, tomato paste, salt at will.
8. Cover and cook on LOW for 25 minutes.
9. Serve hot!
10. Bon Appetite!

Crock Pot Cauliflower Bolognese with Zucchini Noodles

Nothing is so flavor as this vegan cauliflower Bolognese made in the Crock Pot! The cauliflower is engrained with tomato sauce, species, pepper. It is like hearty pasta but without meat. The consistency of cauliflower Bolognese is like a real meat sauce! I'm sure, even those who are not vegan will like this dish.

Ingredients (9 servings):
Preparing for Bolognese:

Cauliflower	1 head
red onion	3/4 cup
garlic	2 small cloves
dried oregano flakes	2 teaspoon
dried basil flakes	1 teaspoon
tomatoes	2 14oz Cans
vegetable broth	1/2 cup
red pepper flakes	1/4 teaspoon
salt and pepper, to taste	

Preparing pasta:

Zucchinis	5 large

Directions:
1. Cut cauliflower into florets.
2. Peel onions and dice. Peel the garlic and mince.
3. Wash zucchini. Make zucchini noodles.
4. Place the cauliflower florets, garlic, onion, oregano, basil, tomatoes, broth, pepper flakes, salt into the Crock Pot.
5. Cover and put on HIGH for 3 hours.
6. Once the Bolognese is done, mash cauliflower with a fork, put over the noodles.
7. Bon Appetite!

Red Thai Veggie Curry

This Thai curry is easy while cooking in the Crock Pot. It could be also cooked with coconut cream, for me, it is better when I use coconut milk. Coconut cream gets the dish creamy and smooth texture, as for me I like the light variant of it. You may also change the soy sauce with a hot one. But don't forget to choose the sauces without sugar.

Ingredients (10 servings):

Cauliflower	1/2 head
Onion	1 small
coconut milk	1 (14 oz.) can
soy sauce	3 tablespoon
sriracha sauce	1-2 teaspoon

salt	1/2 teaspoon
red curry paste	3 tablespoon
sweetener	1 tablespoon
toasted cashews (optional)	1/2 cup
fresh cilantro (optional)	1/4 cup
fresh basil leaves at will	

Directions:
1. Wash and cut cauliflower into florets.
2. Wash cilantro and chop. Set aside.
3. Peel the onion and chop finely.
4. Take a medium bowl, mix coconut milk, both sauces, curry paste, sweetener, pepper, and salt.
5. Pour the mixture into the Crock Pot, add cauliflower and onion. Toss everything together. The veggies must be coated.
6. Cover and put on LOW for 2 hours.
7. Once the dish is done, serve with toasted cashews, chopped cilantro, basil.
8. Bon Appetite!

Spicy Maple Meatballs

The natural Canadian maple syrup together with allspice allows the meatballs be spicy and flavorful. These vegan meatballs are incredible! If you would like to get the one-pot meal you may add a little

(1-2 cups) of vegetable broth or water and get delicious meatball soup.

Ingredients (11 servings):

olive oil	1 tablespoon
white onion	½ pcs
red bell pepper	1 pcs
green bell pepper	1 pcs
jalapeno peppers	2 pcs
plain tomato sauce	1 1/2 cups
maple syrup	1 cup
almond flour	2 tablespoon
ground allspice	2 teaspoon
liquid smoke (optional)	1/8 teaspoon
frozen vegan meatballs	1 bag

Directions:
1. Peel the onion, chop it finely.
2. Wash and take off the seeds from the peppers, slice them. Set aside.
3. Add olive oil to the Crock Pot, add onion and peppers.
4. Take a medium bowl add flour, maple syrup, tomato sauce, allspice, liquid smoke. Mix all

together until smooth consistency. Pour into the Crock Pot.

5. Add frozen meatballs. Cover and cook on LOW for 5 hours.
6. The sauce should be thick and cover the meatballs.
7. Serve warm over cauliflower rice.
8. Bon Appetite!

Crock Pot Spiced Cauliflower

It is a classic Indian cauliflower dish. This hot, flavor dish tingle my taste buds. I can't say I am a fan of cauliflower, but this combination is amazing! You just forget you eat simple cauliflower dish! I think you must also give this dish go. Add your favorite species to this one.

Ingredients (13 servings):

cauliflower	1 large
onion	1 medium pcs
tomato	1 medium
ginger root	1 2-inch piece
garlic	2 cloves
jalapeño peppers	2 pcs
cumin seeds	1 tablespoon
cayenne pepper	1 pinch

garam masala	1 tablespoon
kosher salt	1 tablespoon
turmeric	1 teaspoon
vegetable oil	3 tablespoon
fresh cilantro	1 tablespoon

Directions:

1. Rinse cauliflower, cut into 1-inch pieces.
2. Peel and dice onion.
3. Wash tomato, dry with paper towel, dice.
4. Peel and grate ginger root.
5. Peel and grate the garlic.
6. Remove the seeds from jalapenos, slice.
7. Wash fresh cilantro, chop finely.
8. Put in the Crock Pot cauliflower florets, onion, tomato, ginger, garlic, peppers, masala, salt, turmeric, oil. Stir everything well.
9. Cover and put on LOW for 2 hours.
10. Serve with fresh cilantro.
11. Bon Appetite!

Crock Pot Flavor Brussels Sprouts

This simple dish is appetizing and flavor. This dish includes only 4 simple ingredients (and pine nuts optional. You may also use other nuts you prefer.) All steps you need to do – just to wash the sprouts, put them to the machine and wait. Pour the flavor mixture and that's all!

Ingredients (4 servings):

Brussels sprouts	2 pounds
olive oil	2 tablespoons
salt at will	
pepper optional	
pine nuts at will	
balsamic vinegar	½ cup
sweetener	1-2 tablespoons

Directions:
1. Rinse the sprouts, halve them.
2. Pour olive oil and place sprouts, season them with salt.
3. Cover the Crock Pot, put on LOW for 2 hours.
4. Take a bowl and mix balsamic vinegar with sweetener (like Splenda).
5. Once the veggies are almost done, remove them to a plate and drizzle with the mixture.
6. Dress with toasted pine nuts.
7. Enjoy warm!
8. Bon Appetite!

Crock Pot Keto Ratatouille

I think everyone has eaten ratatouille or has heard about this famous dish at least. This recipe isn't new to you but this is the keto version prepared in the Crock Pot. As for me, I think, it is easier than to cook it in the oven. Just put the ingredients in the Crock Pot and do your business!

Ingredients (7 servings):
sauce

tomato	4 medium
Red sweet pepper	2 small
Garlic	1 clove
Water	1/4 cup
black pepper	

ratatouille

zucchini	1 medium
eggplant	1/2 lb
Green pepper	1 oz

Directions:
1. Prepare the sauce – wash the sweet pepper, take off the seeds, slice.
2. Peel the garlic, chop finely.
3. Wash and crush tomatoes.
4. Blend tomatoes, pepper, salt, garlic, water in a blender. Set aside.
5. Wash and slice zucchini and eggplant.
6. Place veggies into the Crock Pot, pour the sauce.
7. Cover and put on LOW for 2 hours.

8. Bon Appetite!

Crock Pot Butternut Dhal

I'm always happy when the dish is simple to cook and it satisfies my taste buds! This dish is perfect for all my family it comes on our weekly meal plan. One may prepare this in the morning and leave (on WARM) till supper. You may also keep it in the fridge for some days.

Ingredients (10 servings):

red onion	1 pcs
avocado oil	2 tablespoon
garlic purée	1 teaspoon
ginger purée	1 teaspoon
red chili	1 pcs
curry powder	4 teaspoon
coconut milk	3 cups
vegetable stock	1 teaspoon
butternut squash	1 lb
green chili	1 pcs
fresh coriander at will	

Directions:

1. Peel and chop the onion. Take off the seeds from chili, slice.
2. Take a medium saucepan, add oil, fry onions, add garlic and ginger puree, curry and chili. Stir everything well. It takes ca. 5 minutes. Set aside.
3. Wash, peel the butternut squash. Cut it into cubes.
4. Pour this in the Crock Pot, add coconut milk, vegetable stock. Add squash. Season with salt and pepper.
5. Cover and cook on HIGH 3 hours. The consistency must be creamy.
6. Wash the coriander and chop finely.
7. Dress the ready-made dish with fresh coriander.
8. Bon Appetite!

Crock Pot Keto Aubergines

This simple vegan recipe is ideal for busy mornings. You may dress this dish with additional species you prefer, roasted almonds or cashews. One may also use avocado oil or vegetable oil at will. Eat this flavor one warm!

Ingredients (12 servings):

olive oil	4 tablespoon
red onion	1 pcs

garlic	2 cloves
aubergines	1 lb
ripe tomatoes	2 cups
fennel bulb	1 small
sundried tomatoes	½ cup
coriander seeds	1 teaspoon

For the dressing:

Parsley	1/4 cup
Basil	¼ cup
olive oil	2 tablespoon
lemon juice	1 lemon

Directions:

1. Peel the onion and slice.
2. Wash and quarter the tomatoes. Slice fennel.
3. Wash and chop finely the parsley and basil leaves.
4. Squeeze the juice of a lemon.
5. Peel the garlic and crush.
6. Wash the aubergines, slice thinly.
7. Pour the olive oil into the Crock Pot (a half), put onions, garlic, sliced aubergines. Pour the rest of olive oil.

8. Put on the top of the tomatoes, fennel, sundried tomatoes, season with pepper, coriander seeds, salt.
9. Cover and cook on LOW for 5 hours.
10. Combine in a little bowl parsley, basil, olive oil and lemon juice. Whisk everything well.
11. Remove the ready dish to a plate and pour the dressing.
12. Bon Appetite!

Crock Pot Cabbage Soup

If you have some cabbage in the refrigerator, you must definitely cook this cabbage soup. It is very easy and is great for dinner! Simple ingredients that cost not so much and could be found at any store. This keto soup is cooked in the Crock Pot, it means it could be cooked even when you are not at home!

Ingredients (8 servings):

cabbage	1/2 small (4-5 cups)
onion	1 pcs
garlic	4-5 cloves
diced tomatoes	3 1/2 cups
tomato sauce	1 1/2 cups
vegetable broth	4-5 cups
dried parsley	1 tablespoon

oregano   1 teaspoon

salt at will

Directions:
  1. Peel and chop the onion.
  2. Peel the garlic and mince.
  3. Shred the cabbage.
  4. Put cabbage, onion, garlic, sauce, diced tomatoes, broth, oregano, and parsley.
  5. Cover and cook on HIGH 3 hours.
  6. Serve hot.
  7. Bon Appetite!

Keto Creamy Cauliflower Soup

The keto cauliflower soup is definitely easy to cook. The coconut milk adds the creamy texture, it gets light and silk. Serve this soup with fresh basil leaves or chopped parsley, veggie salad or keto bread.

Ingredients (9 servings):

Cauliflower   1 large head

red pepper   3/4 cup (1 medium)

onion   1/2 cup

curry powder   3 teaspoon

fresh ginger   2 teaspoon

salt   1/2 teaspoon

red pepper	1/8 teaspoon
vegetable broth	4 cups
coconut milk	1 14 oz can

Directions:
1. Rinse the cauliflower, cut into about 1 1/2" pieces.
2. Wash and chop the red peppers.
3. Peel the onion, chop finely. Peel the ginger and grate it.
4. Mix florets, pepper, onion, curry, ginger, salt, broth in the Crock Pot. Stir everything well.
5. Cover and put on LOW for 3 hours. The veggies must be tender.
6. Pour the coconut milk and continue cooking 2 hours more.
7. Once the time is over, blend the mixture until smooth.
8. Serve warm.
9. Bon Appetite!

Creamy Roasted Red Pepper Soup

I like this vegan red pepper soup for its color! Bright, sunny, happy soup will make your day today! It is full of the flavor of roasted pepper; coconut milk makes its consistency tender. A combination of shallots, kale, peppers creates a velvety smooth soup.

Ingredients (11 servings):

organic coconut oil	2 tablespoons

red pepper	½ cup
shallot	1 large
celery salt	1 teaspoon
organic paprika	1 teaspoon
red pepper flakes	1 pinch
kale	4 to 5 cups
vegetable stock	4 cups
cider vinegar	1 splash
fresh thyme	1 pinch
coconut milk (canned)	1 cup

Directions:
1. Peel the shallots, chop finely. Chop the kale.
2. Crush the pepper flakes. Wash and remove the seeds from the peppers. Slice them
3. Take a medium saucepan, add oil and put on a high heat.
4. Sautee shallots ca. 2-3 minutes. Add there sliced peppers. Season them well. Roast them ca.3-4 minutes.
5. Add to the Crock Pot the mixture from the saucepan, salt, paprika, pepper flakes, kale, stock, vinegar. Stir everything well.
6. Cover and put on LOW for 2 hours.
7. Add coconut milk, thyme, vinegar and blend everything.

8. Cook another half an hour.
9. Bon Appetite!

Rosemary Garlic Cauliflower Crock Pot

You may ask me, what do we prepare this side dish for? The mashed cauliflower recipe is frequently compared with mashed potatoes. It has a similar texture, consistency and conjoined with similar foods. But wait, it tastes quite different! Cauliflower isn't the same product as a potato. Both taste amazing, but don't forget about your ketogenic diet! I hope you give this recipe a try.

Ingredients (5 servings):

Cauliflower	1 large
fat cream cheese	3 ounces
unsalted butter	2 tablespoons
minced garlic	1 ½ teaspoon
fresh rosemary	1 tablespoon

salt and pepper at will

Directions:
1. Wash the cauliflower, remove the leaves and core, cut it into small pieces (florets).

2. Peel the garlic and mince it. You may saute it if you prefer.
3. Wash the rosemary and chop into small pieces.
4. Open the Crock Pot and put the cauliflower florets into, add a little bit water (1/2 cup), cover and put on LOW for 1 hour.
5. Once the time is ready (the cauliflower florets must be tender), remove them from the Crock Pot and let them cool a little.
6. Put the cooked cauliflower in a food processor or a blender, add fat cream cheese, unsalted butter, minced garlic, chopped rosemary and salt if desired. Blend until smooth texture.
7. Serve cool.
8. Bon Appetite!

Cauliflower Casserole with Tomato and Goat Cheese

I like to cook the dishes that don't need to much time especially if I'm tired after a hard working day! So, today I cook the cauliflower casserole with crumbled Goat cheese and canned tomatoes. It is a perfect casserole, full of vegetables and tastes. Tomatoes, Goat cheese, and cauliflower – what could be easier?

Ingredients (12 servings):
cauliflower florets   6 cups

olive oil	4 teaspoon
dried oregano	1 teaspoon
salt	1/2 teaspoon
ground pepper	1/2 teaspoon
goat cheese crumbled	2 oz.

The Sauce:

olive oil	1 teaspoon
garlic	3 cloves
crushed tomatoes	1 (28 oz.) can
bay leaves	2 pcs
salt	1/4 teaspoon
minced flat-leaf parsley	1/4 cup

Directions:

1. Wash the cauliflower, remove the leaves and core, cut it into small pieces (florets).
2. Spray the bottom of the Crock Pot with cooking spray, put the cauliflower florets on the bottom of it, add olive oil, oregano, and pepper. Salt if desired.
3. Cover and cook on LOW for 2 hours until the cauliflower florets get tender and a little bit brown color.

4. While the cauliflower is cooking prepare the sauce: peel the garlic cloves and mince it. Take a medium-sized skillet, heat the olive oil, add garlic and cook 1 minute, stir it thoroughly all the time.
5. Add the crushed tomatoes and bay leaves, let it simmer for some minutes. Remove the bay leaves, dress with pepper and salt. You may also add parsley if you want.
6. Pour the sauce over the cauliflower florets in the Crock Pot once the time is over.
7. Spread the Goat cheese over the dish, cover the Crock Pot and continue cooking for 1 hour on LOW until the cheese is melted.
8. Serve warm!
9. Bon Appetite!

Cauliflower with Celery Puree And Garlicky Greens

I would like to present you one of my precious purée. It has a creamy combining of tender cauliflower and delicious celery root. This is a quiet combination that is rather tender and delicious when seasoned with a pile of garlicky greens. This time I get excited about this keto side recipe.

Ingredients (8 servings):
For Purée:

celery root   1 medium

cauliflower head	1 small head
salt	1/2 teaspoon
butter	3 tablespoons

For the preparation of Chard:

Swiss chard	2 bunches
Butter	1 tablespoon
garlic cloves	2 small pcs
red pepper flakes	one pinch or 1/8 teaspoon

sea salt at will

Directions:

Prepare the purée:

1. Wash the cauliflower head, remove all green leaves and core, cut it into medium-sized pieces (florets).
2. Peel the celery, cut in little or cubes.
3. Open the Crock Pot, put the celery, cauliflower, put the lid and cook on LOW for 2 hours.
4. Take off the vegetables and place them in the saucepan, conjoin butter, salt and blend thoroughly until puree texture.
5. Dress with salt or pepper if desired. Cover while preparing the garlicky greens and set it aside.

Make the Chard:

1. Stack the leaves of Swiss chard, wash, braid them and slice into 1/3-inch strips. Cut the stems very thinly.
2. Take a skillet, heat the butter in it.
3. Peel the garlic and mince it.
4. Add garlic, pepper flakes. Toss everything for 40 seconds just wait until the garlic is tender.
5. Stir in the leaves of chard, toss it in the butter, garlic for 2-4 minutes.
6. Cover the lid of the skillet and let it cook for 4 minutes until the mixture is tender.
7. Dress with sea salt.
8. Dress the puree with the garlicky greens.
9. Bon Appetite!

Creamy Greek Zucchini Crock Pot

This creamy Greek zucchini side dish is flavor and tender. This recipe is a set of health, spring, color, and taste. I advise you to use only the organic eggs, fresh herbs that you may buy at the farmers' shops and fresh feta cheese. You may also change Feta with the other cheese you prefer more.

Ingredients (9 servings):

zucchini	2 lbs (about 7 large)
organic eggs	2 large
fresh herbs	1 cup
almond meal (or keto breadcrumbs)	1 cup

feta cheese	1 cup
ground cumin	1 teaspoon
fine grain sea salt	1 teaspoon
Ground black pepper at will	
olive oil	3 tablespoons

Directions:

1. Wash zucchini, take off the ends.
2. Put them in a blender and grate.
3. Put the grated zucchini in a medium bowl and season with salt. Leave them to drain for 30 minutes.
4. Take handfuls of the grated zucchini, squeeze all of the moisture. Set aside.
5. Take a medium bowl, beat eggs, add zucchini, cumin, herbs, meal. Mix everything. Add salt, feta, and pepper. Stir well.
6. Place the ready mixture in the refrigerator for 30 minutes.
7. Open the Crock Pot, spread the cooking spray or olive oil over the bottom and sides.
8. Put the mixture into the Crock Pot and set on HIGH for 1 hour.
9. Remove the side dish once the time is over.
10. Serve!

Keto Squash Cake Crock Pot

This keto squash cake or pie (as you like) is a great appetizer and simply easy and low-cost dish. It doesn't need to much time but the variations of eating it are great – you may add mayo, different sauces, both hot and sweet, cheese cream.

Ingredients (9 servings):

Summer squash	1 pound
salt	1 teaspoon
eggs	2 large
scallions	1 1/2 ounce
lemon pepper	1 1/2 teaspoon
baking soda	1/2 teaspoon
almond flour	1/2 cup
coconut flour	1/4 cup
grated Parmesan cheese	1/4 cup

oil for frying

Directions:
1. Wash the squash, dry it with a paper towel.
2. Grate the squash in a food processor. Put the grated squash into a large bowl and sprinkle with salt.
3. Stir the squash gently to spread the salt and let the mixture sit for about 10 minutes.

4. Squeeze the zucchini with hands after this put into a mixing bowl.
5. Add the eggs to the mixture and toss everything.
6. Peel the scallions and chop finely. Mix together with the grated squash.
7. Take a small bowl, stir together lemon pepper, baking soda, almond and coconut flour. Add the mixture to the squash and mix finely altogether.
8. Spray the bottom and the sides of the Crock Pot with cooking spray or oil, pour the mixture into the Crock Pot. Cover and set on LOW for 2 hours.
9. Once the cooking time is over, check the readiness with the toothpick.
10. Remove the squash cake from the Crock Pot on a plate and dress with grated Parmesan cheese.
11. Eat warm.
12. Bon Appetite!

Broccoli and Cheese Stuffed Squash

I can't forget the taste of the broccoli and cheese squash as I tasted it for the first time. I like this dish because of many reasons – this recipe is low in carbohydrates, is cooked rather quickly, tastes delicious, is healthy and simple to prepare. I think everyone who tries it will definitely like it!

Ingredients (7 servings):
squash   1 pcs

broccoli florets	2 cups
garlic	3 pcs
red pepper flakes	1 teaspoon
Italian season	1 teaspoon
mozzarella cheese	1/2 cup
Parmesan cheese	1/3 cup
cooking spray	
salt and pepper at will	

Directions:
1. Wash and dry with a paper towel the squash. Cut in two halves. Take off the seeds. Set aside.
2. Wash broccoli thoroughly and cut into florets.
3. Peel garlic and mince it.
4. Spread the spray over the bottom and the sides of the Crock Pot. Put the halves in the Crock Pot.
5. Add a little bit water of room temperature to the bottom of the Crock Pot.
6. Cover the Crock Pot and put on LOW for about 2 hours, until squash is mild. Check the readiness once the time is over.
7. Take off the squash and let it cool for about 15 minutes.

8. Take a medium skillet, add pepper flakes and a little bit oil and cook for 20 seconds, stir it constantly.
9. Add broccoli, minced garlic to the skillet, continue to stir thoroughly, until the broccoli is tender.
10. Take the squash (previously cooled) and using a fork, take off the flesh of the squash. Add it to the medium bowl and conjoin with the broccoli mixture.
11. Shred carefully the Parmesan cheese, join salt and pepper at will, add seasoning to the mixture. Mix everything well and fill the squash.
12. Put the filled squash again in the Crock Pot, dress with mozzarella cheese each squash half.
13. Add a little bit water if needed to the bottom of the Crock Pot.
14. Cover and cook on LOW for about 1 hour.
15. Remove the dish and enjoy!
16. Bon Appetite!

Roasted Spaghetti Squash and Browned Butter

I know a lot of people who like spaghetti squash like their favorite pasta with tomato sauce. Today I advise you to create spaghetti squash keto-friendly dish that means to conjoin delicious species, butter, and tender squash. All these ingredients on one plate! The butter gets a new taste in this dish.

Ingredients (9 servings):

spaghetti squash	2 pcs
olive oil extra-virgin	1-2 tablespoons
salt	1 teaspoon
black pepper	1 teaspoon
butter	4 tablespoons
hazelnuts	1/4 cup
sage leaves	2 tablespoons
red pepper flakes	1/4 teaspoon
ground cinnamon	1/4 teaspoon

Directions:
1. Wash and dry squash with a paper towel. Cut in two halves. Take off all seeds and set aside.
2. Lightly sprinkle the flesh with oil, add salt at will and pepper.
3. Put the halves into the Crock Pot, cover the lid and set on LOW for 2 hours, squash must be tender.
4. Take off the squash once the time is over and let it cool.
5. Flip the halves carefully. Use a fork, scrape the flesh, try to keep the sides as they are. Set aside.
6. Take a saucepan, put the butter and melt.

7. Cook the butter, whisk carefully all the time until it foams and turns brown and about 2 minutes.
8. Add finely chopped hazelnuts, sage leaves, pepper flakes, cinnamon and continue cooking for about 30 seconds more.
9. Top the butter over the squash.
10. Serve warm.
11. Bon Appetite!

Twice baked Spaghetti Squash Crock Pot

This is the best full spaghetti squash that is so creamy and rich. You need to use your Crock Pot twice during the preparation of this recipe, but be sure it is not so difficult as you think. Try to cook it for the first time and you'll cook it always.

Ingredients (5 servings):

cooked spaghetti squash	2 cups
egg whites	2 pcs
Herbes de Provence	1 teaspoon
Light Swiss Cheese	6 wedges
pinch of salt	
mozzarella cheese	1 cup

Directions:
1. Wash and dry with a paper towel squash.

2. Cut squash in half (lengthwise), remove the seeds.
3. Pour a little bit water into the Crock Pot, put the squash, cover and cook on HIGH for 1 hour. Check the readiness with a fork. Let it cool.
4. Remove the squash, make spaghetti squash. Put them on a plate and add olive oil.
5. Put the cooked spaghetti squash into the bottom of the Crock Pot.
6. Take a bowl, mix egg whites, shredded cheese, seasoning, salt. Blend everything together.
7. Pour the mixture over the spaghetti squash.
8. Season with the rest of cheese.
9. Cover the Crock Pot and set on LOW for 1 hour.
10. Serve warm.
11. Bon Appetite!

Garlic-Parmesan Asparagus Crock Pot

What kind of appetizer could be so flavor as the garlic-Parmesan asparagus? Do you know?! Yes, it is simple but delicious appetizer every beginner could prepare. Everything you need here is just to buy garlic, asparagus, Parmesan and organic fresh eggs. Nothing more!

Ingredients (6 servings):

olive oil extra virgin	2 tablespoons
minced garlic	2 teaspoons

egg	1 pcs fresh
garlic salt	1/2 teaspoon
fresh asparagus	12 ounces
Parmesan cheese	1/3 cup
Pepper at will	

Directions:

1. Peel the garlic and mince it.
2. Wash the asparagus. Shred the Parmesan cheese.
3. Take a medium-sized bowl combine oil, garlic, cracked egg, and salt together. Whisk everything well.
4. Cover the green beans and coat them well.
5. Spread the cooking spray over the bottom of the Crock Pot, put the coated asparagus, season with the shredded cheese. Toss everything finely.
6. Cover and cook on HIGH for 1 hour.
7. Once the time is over you may also season with the rest of the cheese.
8. Bon Appetite!

Keto Asparagus With Soy Sauce

This recipe is quite well for a keto diet. Asparagus is tender, delicious and low in carbs. Don't forget to read the ingredients on a bottle of the soy sauce or just use the coconut aminos. Add this recipe to your private collection of the keto appetizer Crock Pot recipes.

Ingredients (5 servings):

Asparagus	1 lb.
peanut oil	1 tablespoon + 1 teaspoon
soy sauce (sugar-free, keto-friendly)	1 teaspoon
toasted sesame oil	1 teaspoon
sesame seeds	2 teaspoon

Directions:
1. Wash the asparagus.
2. Spray the cooking spray over the bottom of the Crock Pot.
3. Put asparagus on a bottom and sprinkle with oil, turn asparagus in a way it could be coated on all sides.
4. Whisk together the 1 tsp. oil, soy sauce, sesame oil.
5. Cover the Crock Pot and put on HIGH for 1 hour.
6. Once the half an hour is over, open the Crock Pot and sprinkle with the soy mix. Cover again and do the same every 10 minutes.
7. Take off the asparagus from the Crock Pot and dress with toasted sesame seeds.
8. Serve warm.

Garlic butter Keto Spinach

I was always sure that the easiest and delicious recipes are cooked from rather simple ingredients. This appetizer is a great proof of my words. Garlic butter spinach is full of vitamins like C and A, iron, is keto-friendly and tender one!

Ingredients (4 servings):

salted butter	2 tablespoons
garlic, minced	4 cloves
baby spinach	8 oz
Pinch of salt	
lemon juice	1 teaspoon

Directions:
1. Wash the spinach.
2. Peel the garlic cloves and mince finely.
3. Heat up a little skillet, add the butter, melt.
4. Sautee the garlic until a little bit tender.
5. Spray the cooking spray over the bottom of the Crock Pot.
6. Put the spinach into the Crock Pot, season with salt and lemon juice, tender garlic, butter.
7. Cover the Crock pot and put on LOW for 1 hour.
8. Once the time is over, garnish with fresh lemon wedges.
9. Serve hot.

Keto warm Cheese Dip Crock Pot

I began to think about this tasty cheese dip and wished to prepare this amazing one already. I remember as I ate it for the first time. How wonderful was the taste! It's light, easy and corresponds to your ketogenic diet. It is my version of cheese dip, but you might also use your favorite type of cream cheese, also Swiss or Parmesan as an example. Here you are!

Ingredients (6 servings):

Can of chili	1 (15 ounces) pcs
Salsa	1 cup
Cream cheese (room temperature) pkg.	1 (8 ounces)
Cheese (cheddar)	1 cup
Garlic	1 teaspoon minced
Onion	1 clove
Sea salt at will	

Directions:
1. Take your Crock Pot and spray with a non-stick cooking spray that you have at home.
2. Peel the onion and garlic, press the garlic and mince the onion carefully.
3. Open the can of chili and a package of cream cheese (your favorite one), shred the cheddar. Leave a little bit cheddar for serving.

4. Put all the ingredients in the Crock Pot on the bottom and mix well thoroughly with a long spoon.
5. Switch on the Crock Pot and cook on LOW for about 4 hours. Another saying, until the Crock Pot completely heated. Stir occasionally during cooking. I made it 2-3 times.
6. Stir carefully before serving once more, right before time ends.
7. Top your cheese dip with green onions at will and the rest of cheddar.
8. You may also eat with veggies.
9. Bon Appetite!

Kale, Spinach, Artichoke Dip Crock Pot

Oh dear, don't you know the easiest and the most delicious dip prepared in the Crock Pot? Haven't you tried it yet? Traditional artichoke, as well as spinach in a mixture of kale and other ingredients, could make a perfect addition to your keto diet! If you don't like kale or spinach, you may prepare it without these ingredients. This dip is very scrummy pasta sauce eating with keto bread. It is highly recommended here to use the Parmesan cheese of high quality! You'll taste the difference

Ingredients (11 servings):

Garlic	2 cloves
Onion	½ cup

Artichoke	28 oz canned
spinach	10 oz
kale	10 oz
Parmesan cheese	1 cup
Mozzarella	1 cup
Greek yogurt	1 cup
sour cream	3/4 cup
mayonnaise	1/4 cup

Salt and pepper to taste

Directions:
1. Peel the onion, garlic and chop everything into pieces.
2. Put garlic, onion, and artichokes in the food processor and mix together.
3. Wash spinach and chop it. Chop the kale, grate Parmesan cheese, cut the mozzarella cheese.
4. Add the mixture of garlic, onion, and artichokes in the Crock Pot and stir together.
5. Add cheese, mozzarella, mayo, sour cream, Greek yogurt, kale, spinach to the mixture in the Crock Pot.
6. Cover the Crock Pot and cook for 4 hours on HIGH.
7. Season the ready dish with salt and pepper at will.

8. Bon Appetite!

Keto Crock Pot Glazed Walnuts

If you are a great lover of short but tasty and healthy snakes or appetizer this will surely be among your favorites. It is simple to prepare just some buttons on the Crock Pot, a little number of ingredients - only walnuts, butter, maple syrup and vanilla extract - and a keto glazed maple walnuts on your table!

Ingredients (4 servings):

Walnuts   16 ounces

Butter   ½ cup

Maple syrup (unsweetened)   ½ cup

Vanilla extract   1 slop-feeder

Directions:
1. Put the walnuts, butter, maple syrup and vanilla extract into the Crock Pot.
2. Turn the Crock Pot on LOW and cook for 2 hours.
3. Stir every 25 minutes to be sure, all the walnuts are covered and not burned.
4. After the time is over, take the walnuts off and cool on a parchment paper.
5. Eat as appetizer or store in a Ziploc bag.

Crock Pot Keto «English Muffin»

I think the majority of us have heard this word combination - «English muffin». Don't be surprised that we cook it today in the Crock Pot and as a result, we get one, a large muffin that we could cut with a knife and eat like small muffins from the usual oven Cooking in the Crock Pot doesn't need too much time as in the oven. Try to cook this following my easy instructions!

Ingredients (6 servings):

Almond flour   3 tablespoon

Coconut flour   1/2 tablespoon

Butter (or coconut oil)   1 tablespoon

Egg   1 large

Sea salt   1 pinch

baking soda   1/2 teaspoon

salt at will

Directions:
1. Take a medium-sized skillet, melt the butter. It takes usually 20-30 seconds.
2. Take to the skillet with melted butter coconut and almond flour, egg, salt and stir everything well.
3. Take from the heat and add baking soda.
4. Open the Crock Pot, spray the bottom of the Crock Pot with cooking spray. Pour the mixture.

5. Cover the lid and put on LOW for 2 hours. Check the readiness with a fork.
6. Remove the baked «muffin» from the Crock Pot and eat with bacon slices, cheese or other ingredients.
7. Bon Appetite!

Crustless Crock Pot Spinach Quiche

This crustless spinach quiche is perfectly well for the breakfast both for adults and kids. It is easy, keto-friendly, cheep and quickly. It doesn't take you too much time to prepare this quiche. Add your favorite species once the dish is ready.

Ingredients (11 servings):

frozen spinach	10 oz package
butter or ghee	1 tablespoon
red bell pepper	1 medium
Cheddar cheese	1 1/2 cups
eggs	8 pcs
homemade sour cream	1 cup
fresh chives	2 tablespoons
sea salt	1/2 teaspoon
ground black pepper	1/4 teaspoon
ground almond flour	1/2 cup

baking soda   1/4 teaspoon

Directions:

1. Let the frozen spinach thaw and drain it well. Chop finely.
2. Wash the pepper and slice it. Take off the seeds.
3. Shred the cheddar cheese and set aside.
4. Chop finely the fresh chives.
5. Open the Crock Pot and spray the bottom and sides with cooking spray.
6. Take a little skillet, heat the butter over high heat, sautee pepper until tender, about 6 minutes.
7. In a large bowl combine together eggs, sour cream, salt, pepper.
8. Add grated cheese and chives and continue to mix.
9. In another medium-sized bowl, mix together almond flour with baking soda. Pour into the egg mixture, add peppers in the eggs mixture, pour gently into the Crock Pot.
10. Cover the lid and set on high for 2 hours.
11. Bon Appetite!

Pot Turkish Breakfast Eggs

Turkish-style breakfast is low-calories, keto-friendly, full of vitamin C and tasty dish for early morning. Begin your daily routine with full energy, smile, green veggies, hot species and a good mood. Let's enjoy this recipe together!

Ingredients (9 servings):

olive oil	1 tablespoon
onions	2 pcs
red pepper	1 pcs
red chili	1 small
cherry tomatoes	8 pcs
keto bread	1 slice
eggs	4 pcs
milk	2 tablespoon
small bunch of parsley	
natural yogurt at will	4 tablespoon
pepper at will	

Directions:
1. Peel the onions and chop finely.
2. Wash parsley and chop finely. Wash the cherry tomatoes and dry with a paper towel.
3. Wash the pepper and chili, take off the seeds from the bell pepper and slice.
4. Cube the keto bread.
5. Spray the inside of the Crock Pot with oil or cooking spray.
6. In a large skillet, heat the oil, add the onions, pepper, and chili. Stir everything together.
7. Cook until the veggies begin to soften.

8. Put them in the Crock Pot and add the cherry tomatoes and bread, stir everything well.
9. Cover and cook on LOW for 4 hours.
10. Season with fresh parsley and yogurt.
11. Bon Appetite!

Persian Omelet Crock Pot

This vegetarian recipe is full of fresh sunny herbs, green onions, organic eggs and pine nuts. This recipe is cooked until golden brown. I usually top it with the Greek yogurt but you may also add the sour cream.

Ingredients (14 servings):

olive oil	2 tablespoon
butter	1 tablespoon
red onion	1 large
green onions	4 pcs
garlic	2 cloves
spinach	2 oz
fresh chives	¼ cup
cilantro leaves	¼ cup
parsley leaves	¼ cup
fresh dill	2 tablespoon

Kosher salt and black pepper at will

pine nuts   ¼ cup

eggs   9 large

whole milk   ¼ cup

Greek yogurt at will 1 cup

Directions:
1. Peel the onion cut thinly.
2. Chop carefully green onions. Chop chives.
3. Wash spinach after this carefully chops it.
4. Peel garlic and mince.
5. Finely cut cilantro and parsley, dill.
6. Take a saucepan melt the butter. Add red onion, stirring occasionally, it takes about 8-9 min.
7. Add green onions, garlic, continue cooking for 4 minutes.
8. Put the spinach, chives, parsley, cilantro, add salt and pepper at will. Remove the skillet, add the pine nuts.
9. Take a bowl, crack the eggs, add milk and a little pepper and whisk.
10. Mix the eggs with veggie mixture.
11. Open the Crock Pot and spread the cooking spray over the bottom and sides. Pour the mix into the Crock Pot.
12. Cover the lid and put on LOW for 3 hours. Serve with Greek yogurt.
13. Bon Appetite!

Crock Pot Cream Cheese French toast

Keto cream-cheese French toasts are great at the beginning of the day. Light keto bread slices, covered with cream mixture in a combination with almonds are delicious and amazing! I usually dress these toasts with maple syrup.

Ingredients (9 servings):

cream cheese	1 (8-oz) package
slivered almonds	¼ cup
keto bread	1 loaf
eggs	4 pcs
almond extract	1 teaspoon
sweetener	1 teaspoon
milk	1 cup
butter	2 teaspoon
Cheddar cheese	½ cup

Maple syrup, at will, for dressing

Directions:
1. Take a large bowl, mix together cream cheese with almonds.
2. Slice the keto bread into 2-inch slices. Try to make a 1/2-inch slit (horizontal) in the bottom of every slice to make a pocket.
3. Fill all the slices with cream mixture. Set aside.

4. In a little bowl mix eggs, extract the sweetener in milk. Coat the keto slices into the mix.
5. Open the Crock Pot and spread the cooking spray over the bottom and sides.
6. Put the coated keto slices on the bottom of the Crock Pot. Put on the top of each separate slice additional shredded cheese.
7. Cover the lid and put on LOW for 2 hours.
8. Serve hot.
9. Bon Appetite!

Crock Pot Broccoli Omelet

Do you prefer to have some eggs for a breakfast? The broccoli omelet could be a great addition to your morning herbal tea or coffee that doesn't need to much time and a lot of ingredients. I think you have all the ingredients in your refrigerator.

Ingredients (14 servings):

Eggs	6 large
fat milk	1/2 cup
Salt	1/4 teaspoon
Pepper	1/2 teaspoon
garlic powder	1/4 teaspoon
chili powder	1/4 teaspoon

shortening or non-stick cooking spray (for greasing the crockpot)

yellow onion	1 pcs small
garlic	3 cloves
fresh broccoli florets	1 cup
parmesan cheese	1 tablespoon
cheddar cheese	1 - 2 cups
tomato chopped	1 pcs medium
green onions	1/4 cup

Directions:
1. Peel the yellow onion and cut it. Peel the garlic and press, shred the cheese and wash the medium red tomato, dry with paper towel and cut also. Chop the green onions.
2. Take a cooking spray and spread it over the bottom and all the sides of your Crock Pot, just to prevent sticking.
3. Crack the eggs into a large bowl, add the cup of milk mix well, add all the species and mix it once more carefully.
4. Add the onions to the mixture, then garlic, Parmesan cheese, and broccoli florets. Continue whisking it thoroughly.
5. Put your mixture into the Crock Pot, cover and cook on HIGH for 2 hours.
6. As soon as the time is over, with using the long keen knife cut along the edge of the Crock Pot into quarters.

7. Take your omelet to the plate and serve with remaining cheddar and green chopped onions.
8. Bon Appetite!

Keto Pumpkin Spice Pie

This keto Crock Pot pumpkin pie recipe is great! I can't quite decide if it's pie or if it's bread. It is well in both situations, depending on how you treat this after it is ready. Eat it in the morning and you'll get a wonderful full breakfast meal. In another way, it is delicious at any time.

Ingredients:

raw pecans	1 1/2 cups
Swerve Sweetener	3/4 cup
coconut flour	1/3 cup
unflavoured whey protein powder	1/4 cup
baking powder	2 teaspoon
ground cinnamon	1 1/2 teaspoon
ground ginger	1 teaspoon
ground cloves	1/4 teaspoon
salt	1/4 teaspoon
pumpkin puree	1 cup
eggs	4 large

butter melted	1/4 cup
vanilla extract	1 teaspoon

Directions:

1. Spread the bottom of the Crock Pot with cooking spray.
2. Grind the pecans in the food processor until the coarse meal, but don't let turn them into the butter.
3. Transfer pecans to the bowl and whisk together, add coconut flour, sweetener, baking powder, whey protein powder, ginger, cinnamon, salt garlic and whisk once more.
4. Mix in another bowl pumpkin puree, cracked eggs, vanilla, butter until well mixed.
5. Join everything together, add this mixture to the Crock Pot and set on LOW for 3 hours.
6. As soon as the top of the pie is barely firm to the touch the pumpkin spice pie is ready.
7. Bon Appetite!

Keto Crock Pot Gingerbread

Among my preferred bread recipes is also a gingerbread, but it almost for those who like it. This recipe includes a variety of species for those who are great lovers.

Ingredients (13 servings):

almond flour	2 1/4 cups

Swerve Sweetener	3/4 cup
coconut flour	2 tablespoon
ground ginger	1 1/2 tablespoon
ground cinnamon	1/2 tablespoon
baking powder	2 teaspoon
ground cloves	1/2 teaspoon
salt	1/4 teaspoon
butter melted	1/2 cup
eggs	4 pcs
milk	2/3 cup
freshly squeezed lemon juice	1 tablespoon
vanilla extract	1 teaspoon

Directions:
1. Spread the bottom and the sides of the Crock Pot with the butter or cooking spray.
2. Shred the ginger, peel the cloves and press.
3. Take a large bowl, add the almond flour, sweetener, shredded ginger, coconut flour, cinnamon, salt and baking powder, pressed cloves.
4. Mix in another little bowl melted butter, milk, cracked eggs, lemon juice and vanilla extract.

5. Combine everything together from the first and second bowls.
6. Put everything into the Crock Pot, cook on LOW for 3 hours.
7. Let it cool a little!
8. Bon Appetite!

Keto Crock Pot Mediterranean Frittata

What kind of dish looks like super tasty and doesn't need too much time for breakfast? Yah, it is the keto Crock Pot Mediterranean frittata! You just put all the vegetables into the Crock Pot, pour the eggs mixture and make your business. In the morning you have a great breakfast at the table!

Ingredients (8 servings):

Eggs	8 pcs
Almond milk	⅓ cup
dried oregano	1 teaspoon
Salt and freshly ground black pepper at will	
baby arugula	4 cups
red peppers	1¼ cups
red onion	½ cup
goat cheese	¾ cup

Directions:
1. Peel the onion and slice it thinly.
2. Crumble the goat cheese.
3. Take a medium bowl, crack the eggs into it, add milk, oregano and combine. Add pepper and salt at will.
4. Put the roasted red pepper, baby arugula, goat cheese and onion into the Crock Pot. Pour the eggs mixture over vegetables.
5. Cover and cook on LOW for 3 hours.
6. Serve the dish immediately.
7. Bon Appetite!

Crock-Pot Keto Artichoke, Spinach

An easy keto recipe with artichoke hearts and frozen spinach is light and hearty. It updates your usual boring morning breakfast with balmy relish. You may serve it with vegetables or keto bread.

Ingredients (6 servings):

jarred artichoke hearts	14 - 15 ounces
spinach (frozen)	10 ounces
cream cheese	8 ounces
Parmesan cheese	1 cup
Garlic	3 cloves
Sea salt and pepper at will	

Directions:

1. Peel the garlic, mince it.
2. Grate the cheese.
3. Prepare the frozen spinach, don't defrost them.
4. Drain half of the liquid from the jarred artichokes.
5. Conjoin all the components – artichoke, spinach, cream cheese, Parmesan, minced garlic in the Crock Pot. Savour sea salt and pepper at will.
6. Cap and cook on LOW for two hours. The cheese must be melted.
7. Stir from time to time.
8. Serve with keto bread or vegetables.

Greek Eggs Breakfast Casserole

I'd like to present you here an amazing mixture of vegetables, Feta cheese, and eggs! Try to taste the Greek eggs breakfast casserole and I'm sure it will be among your favorites forever!

Ingredients (9 servings):

eggs (whisked)	12 pcs
milk	½ cup
salt	½ teaspoon
black pepper	1 teaspoon
Red Onion	1 tablespoon

Garlic	1 teaspoon
Sun-dried tomatoes	½ cup
spinach	2 cups
Feta Cheese	½ cup
pepper at will	

Directions:

1. Peel the onion and garlic and cut them (you may also press the garlic). Cut the spinach. Crush Feta cheese in a little plate.
2. Take a bowl, crack the eggs and whisk them thoroughly.
3. Add to the mixture milk, pepper, salt and stir to combine.
4. Add there minced onion and garlic.
5. Add dried tomatoes and spinach.
6. Pour all the mixture into the Crock Pot, add Feta cheese.
7. Cover and cook on LOW 5-6 hours.
8. Bon Appetite!

Keto Pumpkin and Coconut Soup

Do you know the recipe how to prepare an easy keto coconut and pumpkin soup? Not yet? I will tell you the easiest and cheapest way to cook it. This soup prepared quickly in the Crock Pot is super winter warmer one! Moreover, you may freeze this tasty soup in small baking dishes (for example for baking of muffins in portions) and re-heat when you wish.

Ingredients (7 servings):

Yellow onion	1 pcs medium
ginger	1 teaspoon
garlic	1 teaspoon
butter	55 g
pumpkin chunks	500 g
vegetable stock	500 ml
coconut cream	400 ml

salt and pepper to taste

Directions:
1. Peel and dice the onion, after this garlic and mince it (or press – as you wish).
2. Peel the ginger and crush it.
3. Wash and cut the pumpkin. Take off the seeds.
4. Put all the ingredients into the Crock Pot – diced onions, garlic, butter, vegetable stock, pepper and salt at will, pumpkin chunks, crushed ginger.
5. Cover and cook on LOW for 6-7 hours or on HIGH for 5-6 hours.
6. After the time is over, take the cover off, puree the mixture in the blender until smooth consistency.

7. Put on WARM until ready and serve!
8. Garnish with coconut cream.
9. Bon Appetite!

Crock Pot Acorn Squash Soup

Today, I decided finally to cook acorn squash soup. This is delicious, vegan, healthy soup that is rather easy to cook even for beginners. I decided to add a little bit cayenne pepper, just to accent the natural tastes of acorn squashes.

Ingredients (13 servings):

acorn squashes	3 pcs
sea salt	1 teaspoon
ground black pepper	1 teaspoon
olive oil	2 tablespoon
shallot	1 pcs
yellow onion	½ pcs
red onion	½ pcs
dried ginger	1/2 teaspoon
dried sage	1/4 teaspoon
cayenne pepper	1/8 teaspoon
ground allspice	1/8 teaspoon
vegetable stock	4 cups

water   1 cup

Directions:

1. Peel the shallot, yellow and red onion, wash and chop everything finely.
2. Sprinkle the ready prepared cut acorn squashes with salt and pepper, put them into the Crock Pot, add a cup of water, cover and cook on LOW for 5 hours.
3. Remove the squash once the time is over, let it cool.
4. Remove flesh from acorns' skin using a spoon into the medium bowl.
5. Mix everything in a large bowl: Chopped onions, shallot, ginger, olive oil, cayenne pepper and stir everything. Add squash flesh and vegetable broth.
6. Cover and cook on LOW for 2 hours. Add dried sage.
7. Using a food processor or a blender make a puree mixture.
8. Once the puree is ready, add pepper and salt to taste. Eat warm.
9. Bon Appetite!

Keto Maple Custard

An easy keto maple custard could be cooked using the maple syrup but it could be changed easily to another preferred one. As for me, I prefer Sukrin Gold as a sugar replacement that corresponds to a keto diet. Of course, you may use the other replacement if you want.

Ingredients (8 servings):

eggs' yolks	2 egg
heavy cream (Horizon Organic)	1 cup
milk	1/2 cup
Sukrin Gold (or other sugar substitutes)	1/4 cup
maple extract	1 teaspoon
salt	1/4 teaspoon
cinnamon	1/2 teaspoon

Directions:
1. Prepare the eggs' yolks. Conjoin them with heavy cream, Sukrin Gold, salt maple extract, cinnamon. Mix or stir everything carefully.
2. Spread the Crock Pot with cooking spray or grease if you have such one, fill the Crock Pot with the mixture.
3. Cover the mixture and cook on LOW for 2 hours.
4. The maple custard must be jiggly after 2 hours.
5. Enjoy the maple custard with whipped cream!

6. Bon Appetite!

Chapter 2; Lunch Recipes

Avocado Toad in the Hole

Such a cute name for a simple lunch. First time when I heard this recipe I thought it must be something with bread. But I think eating avocado is healthier than eating bread. Moreover, you get a great quantity of fat at the first part of the day, set of vitamin and good mood.

Ingredients (6 servings):

avocados	3 medium pcs
eggs	6 medium
garlic powder	1 teaspoon
sea salt	1/2 teaspoon
black pepper	1/4 teaspoon
Parmesan cheese	1/4 cup

Directions:

1. Wash and cut in half avocados, remove the pits. Scoop out about 1/4 of the meat from each part. You must create enough space to fit the egg inside.

2. Open the Crock Pot and spray the cooking spray over the bottom.
3. Place the halves of avocado into a bottom of the Crock Pot.
4. Sprinkle each part with salt, garlic powder, and black pepper.
5. Grate the Parmesan cheese.
6. Crack the fresh egg into each part of the avocado and sprinkle with cheese over the tops of the eggs.
7. Cover the Crock Pot and put on HIGH for 1 hour.
8. The egg whites must be no longer jiggles.
9. Eat warm.
10. Bon Appetite!

Japanese Pumpkin Dip

Today I say «Hello» to this delicious and tasty Japanese pumpkin dip. You don't need to rise to Japan or Thailand to taste this amazing and colorful dip. Everything you need – to follow my instructions strictly, be patient and get a super tasty, light dip for lunch!

Ingredients (11 servings):

Japanese pumpkin	3 lbs
olive oil	1/4 cup
sea salt	1 teaspoon
white onion	1 medium

unsalted butter (or ghee)   2 tablespoon

heavy cream (or coconut cream) 2 cups

garlic powder   1 tablespoon

sea salt   1 teaspoon

fresh rosemary   4 sprigs

water or broth   1/2 - 1 cup

pumpkin seeds   1/3 cup

Directions:
1. Wash the Japanese pumpkin and remove the seeds.
2. Chop into 2-inch cubes.
3. Open the Crock Pot and spray the cooking spray over the bottom.
4. Put the cubes on a bottom of the Crock Pot, drizzle with olive oil and season with salt. Cover and put on HIGH for 2 hours.
5. Peel chop finely the white onion cooks it until golden in a little saucepan with unsalted butter.
6. Once the onion is translucent, put it into a bowl. Set aside.
7. Blend heavy cream in a food processor for about 5 minutes.
8. Add the cooked onion, garlic powder, salt and fresh rosemary. Blend everything well.
9. Once the pumpkin is ready, let cool a little and peel the skin off. Blend the peeled pumpkin into the food processor until creamy.

10. Transfer the pumpkin soup to the Crock Pot and put on LOW for 1 more hour.
11. Serve with pumpkin seeds!
12. Enjoy warm!

Blackberry Egg Keto Bake

This recipe is absolutely for those why are lazy but still, like to enjoy something tasty and unusual. It requires very little time to make and is pretty delicious. This recipe includes an unusual flavor combination and the texture. The rosemary, lime zest and ginger combined together with a little bit vanilla give the eggs a refreshing backdrop to the fresh blackberries.

Ingredients (9 servings):

Eggs	5 large
butter (melted)	1 tablespoon
coconut flour	3 tablespoons
grated fresh ginger	1 teaspoon
vanilla	1/4 teaspoon
fine sea salt	1/3 teaspoon
zest of lime	1/2 tablespoon
fresh rosemary	1 teaspoon
cup fresh blackberries	½ cup

Directions:
1. Open the Crock Pot and spray the cooking spray over the bottom.
2. Melt the butter in a little saucepan.
3. Chop finely fresh rosemary.
4. Place freshly cracked eggs, melted butter, coconut flour, freshly grated ginger, vanilla, salt, zest into a blender and process about two minutes on high. The mixture must be fully combined and smooth.
5. Add the rosemary and pulse a few times until rosemary is just combined.
6. Put the egg mixture into the Crock Pot add blackberries there.
7. Cover the Crock Pot and set on HIGH for 1 hour, until the egg mixture puffs and is fully cooked through.
8. Let it cool for some minutes once the cooking time is over. Add chopped rosemary.
9. Bon Appetite!

Quick Sausage Lunch for Two

Quick sausage lunch is great because you put all the ingredients in the Crock Pot and let it cook. Today I decided to combine the robust flavors of vegetarian sausages with full of carbs with species, ketchup, and veggies. A plenty of melted cheese will never damage your dish!

Ingredients (9 servings):

Vegetarian sausages	5 pcs
white onion	1 tablespoon
ketchup	1/2 cup
Parmesan cheese	1/4 cup
shredded mozzarella	1/4 cup
oregano	1/2 teaspoon
basil	1/2 teaspoon
salt	1/4 teaspoon
red pepper	1/4 teaspoon

Directions:
1. Open the Crock Pot and spray the cooking spray over the bottom.
2. Cut the vegetarian sausages into rounds (about 1/2 inch) and put them to the Crock Pot.
3. Shred mozzarella and Parmesan cheese.
4. Peel and finely dice the onion. Add to the Crock Pot also.
5. Pour the ketchup and Parmesan cheese. Stir to combine everything well.
6. Add onion, oregano, pepper, and salt. Cover the Crock Pot and set on LOW for 2 – 3 hours.
7. Once the cooking time is over, open the Crock Pot and sprinkle with mozzarella cheese.
8. Sprinkle with basil.

9. Bon Appetite!

Shakshuka Keto Crock Pot

This dish can be enjoyed together with all your family and friends or you may eat it alone. It's essentially a sauce made of tomatoes and finely chopped chili peppers. If you are bored of the usual scrambled eggs prepared for lunches, this can be a great alternative. Enjoy preparing your sauce if you have a plenty of time and a really awesome recipe. This time I decided to use one of my favorite marinara sauces.

Ingredients (7 servings):

marinara sauce	1 cup
pepper	1 chili
eggs	4 pcs
feta cheese	1 oz
cumin	1/8 teaspoon
salt	
pepper	
fresh basil (at will)	
or fresh oregano (if desired)	

Directions:
1.   Finely chop the chili. But be careful!

2. Take a medium-sized bowl and add a cup of marinara sauce, chopped chili. Whisk everything together

3. Crack fresh eggs to the marinara and chili mixture, continue whisking.

4. Crumble the feta cheese and sprinkle it over the marinara-eggs mix, season this with pepper and salt at will. Add cumin.

5. Open the Crock Pot and spray the cooking spray over the bottom.

6. Pour the mix into the Crock Pot, cover and set on LOW for 2 hours. Check the dish from time to time, it must seem not cooked enough rather to heat itself.

7. Once the time is over, the eggs must be still runny a little. Transfer the shakshuka from the Crock Pot on a plate carefully, helping with spoon or blade.

8. Wash and chop fresh basil, sprinkle it over the ready dish.

9. Enjoy!

Keto Feta & Pesto Omelet

This keto omelet is absolutely great for a season of fresh and flavor basil. This time pesto must be on the menu, of course, if you like it. That's why I decided to cook this quick Italian lunch and namely pesto and feta omelet. The end result I became after mixing all these simple and delicious ingredients was really great. I don't want even describe this sunny, delicate and herby pesto omelet but wish you cook it quickly.

Ingredients (5 servings):

Butter	1 tablespoon
Eggs	5 pcs
heavy cream	1 tablespoon
feta cheese	1 oz.
pesto	1 tablespoon
salt	
pepper	

Directions:
1. Take a medium-sized saucepan and heat it up. Melt a tablespoon of butter.
2. Take another little bowl, crack the fresh eggs, add melted butter and put a tablespoon of heavy cream. (If you want to get your omelet fluffy).
3. Open the Crock Pot and spray the cooking spray over the bottom.
4. Pour the eggs mix into the Crock Pot and put on LOW for 1-1,5 hours until fully cooked.
5. Once the time is almost over, open the Crock Pot and sprinkle pesto on the top of the dish.
6. Shred the feta cheese and spread it over the top of the omelet also.

7. Cover the Crock Pot and wait until the feta cheese is fully melted over the omelet.
8. Once the feta is melted, transfer the ready dish on a plate carefully and season with salt and pepper.
9. Garnish with more feta at will and fresh basil leaves if desired or cherry tomatoes.
10. Bon Appetite!

Avocado Fries Crock Pot

Have searched for amazing quick lunch recipes? You have found the recipe you must cook for sure! Simple to make, keto-friendly, quick and flavor! Crispy outside and tender inside. Every beat of this tasty lunch is full of fat, so you will not feel hunger the rest of the day! If you don't like sriracha hot sauce, feel free to prepare the other one like garlic dip or cilantro lime dip.

Ingredients (8 servings):
Fries

Avocados	3 pcs
Egg	1 pcs
almond meal	1 1/2 cups
sunflower oil	1 1/2 cups
cayenne pepper	1/4 teaspoon
salt	1/2 teaspoon

Spicy Mayo

homemade mayo	2 tablespoons
sriracha	2 tablespoons

Directions:
1. Take a medium-sized bowl, crack a fresh egg into this bowl, whisk it thoroughly.
2. Tae another medium bowl, join the almond meal with a little bit salt and cayenne pepper.
3. Wash and slice avocados in half, carefully take out the seeds.
4. Peel off the skin off every half.
5. Slice each slice of avocado 4 or 5 pieces (if it is rather big).
6. Open the Crock Pot and sunflower oil to the bottom of the Crock Pot.
7. Coat each of avocado slices the egg mixture.
8. Put each avocado slice in the almond meal carefully, do this until you will not fully see the avocado green.
9. Place each covered slice of avocado into the Crock Pot.
10. Cover and put on HIGH for 2 hours. Turn the slices from time to time.
11. Once the cooking time is over, transfer slices quickly to a plate.
12. In a little bowl, mix sriracha sauce and mayo and deep the avocado slices before eating!
13. Enjoy hot!

Crock Pot Yorkshire Pudding

Cooking a keto Yorkshire pudding in the Crock Pot? Not a problem! Flavor, tender and fully amazing! Perfect meal for lunch is today on your table! Enjoy immediately once the pudding is ready.

Ingredients (15 servings):

refined avocado oil	¼ cup
eggs	4 large
whole milk or 2% milk	2 cups
almond flour	2 cups
salt	½ teaspoon
grated nutmeg	⅛ teaspoon

Filling

Roma tomatoes	2 pcs
mozzarella	12 mini
eggs, any size	5 pcs

Topping

Avocado	1 pcs
green onion, diced	1 pcs
olive oil	1 tablespoon
lemon juice	2 teaspoon

chili flakes	¼ teaspoon
salt	¼ teaspoon

Directions:
1. Take a large bowl, whisk freshly cracked eggs with milk. Season with salt, flour, and nutmeg. Mix thoroughly. Set aside.
2. Place the oiled base in the Crock Pot (it must be covered with cooking spray previously) and bake for 2 hours until softened.
3. While the base is cooking prepare the filling: wash the tomatoes, take off the seeds and cut into pieces.
4. Cube the mozzarella cheese.
5. In the hole of the prepared base, put diced tomatoes and mozzarella. Crack fresh eggs.
6. Put the pudding again into the Crock Pot and set on LOW for 1 hour or until yolks are still a little bit runny.
7. Prepare the topping: take a small bowl, peel and dice avocado, green onion, salt, chili flakes, olive oil, lemon juice.
8. Once the pudding is ready, remove it from the Crock Pot and top with the avocado mix.
9. Serve immediately.
10. Bon Appetite!

Crock Pot Scrambled Eggs with Green Herbs

I cook these eggs in the Crock Pot to get them a velvety and delicious, tender texture. This recipe is great – I put all the ingredients into the Crock Pot, set on LOW and do my private business. Once the cooking time is over I have a perfect light lunch!

Ingredients (8 servings):

Eggs	10 extra-large
whole milk	6 tablespoons
kosher salt	1 teaspoon
black pepper	½ teaspoon
parsley leaves	2 tablespoons
scallions	2 tablespoons
fresh dill	2 tablespoons
unsalted butter	2 tablespoons

Directions:
1. Wash fresh parsley leaves. Chop them finely and set aside.
2. Peel the scallions, cut finely.
3. Wash the fresh dill and mince it also.
4. Take a medium-sized bowl, whisk together milk, eggs, salt, pepper, scallions, parsley, and dill.
5. Melt the butter in an omelet pan.

6. Mix the egg mix with butter and pour into the Crock Pot.
7. Cover the lid of the Crock Pot and put on LOW for 1-2 hours.
8. Serve hot.
9. Bon Appetite!

Crock Pot Tart with Butternut Squash and Kale

I don't know the lighter tart prepared in the Crock Pot following all the keto rules than this one! The base is tender and delicious, despite the butter in the base, it is far less than the traditional type. It is in crumbly, flavor and amazing!

Ingredients (11 servings):
Base cooking:

almond flour	1 cup
sea salt	1 teaspoon
sprigs fresh thyme	
butter, cold	½ cup
ice-cold water	4 - 6 tablespoons
beaten egg	1pcs

Filling

olive oil	2 tablespoon

red onion	1pcs
butternut squash	1 pcs
kale	1 cup
sea salt and black pepper	
organic eggs	3 pcs
whole milk	1 cup
nutmeg, for grating	
Gruyere cheese	½ cup

Directions:

Base:

1. Prepare the base using hands: mix the flour, salt, thyme altogether.
2. Add butter and continue mixing thoroughly.
3. Add water, whisk all the time, until all the ingredients come together.
4. Make a circle with the same diameter as your Crock Pot, and put into the refrigerator for 1 hour.
5. Once the time is over, roll the base, sprinkle the bottom and the walls of the Crock Pot with cooking spray and put it inside.
6. Prepare the filling: peel and cut finely the onion.
7. Peel and grate the squash, take off the stalks from kale and chop the leaves. Grate the cheese on a plate.

8. Take a medium-sized skillet, heat the oil and add onion, cook until soft and sweet.
9. Add squash, kale, season with salt and pepper. Stir well. Set aside.
10. Take a little bowl, break the eggs and whisk them. Pour the milk over the eggs and whisk all together, then add salt and pepper, nutmeg. Mix together.
11. Once the veggies are cool, add the egg mixture and whisk well.
12. Pour the mix into the base and set on HIGH for 2 hours.
13. Serve hot!
14. Bon Appetite!

Ginger and Turmeric Keto Dip

The tender and healthy dip with broccoli, ginger, and turmeric is full of healthy components and rather warm for a windy day. It is amazing for lunch, busy day when you don't have time to cook the amazing dishes consisting of a huge amount of the components.

Ingredients (8 servings)

Butter	2 teaspoon
leeks	4 cups
ginger	2 teaspoon
broccoli florets	8 cups

ground turmeric	1 teaspoon
salt	1 teaspoon
pinch of black pepper	
sesame oil	1 teaspoon
stock	6 cups

Directions:

1. Wash and chop the leeks.
2. Peel and grate the ginger.
3. Chop the broccoli florets.
4. Take a large saucepan over high heat, melt the butter.
5. Add the leeks, cook, toss well, leeks must be cooked through.
6. Put the leeks in the Crock Pot, add grated ginger, broccoli florets, turmeric, pepper, salt, sesame oil.
7. Add broth and toss well.
8. Cover the lid of the Crock Pot, cook on HIGH for 2 hours. Broccoli must be tender.
9. Use a blender, mix until smooth.
10. Serve with yogurt.

Crock Pot Keto Kale Gratin

When it comes to lunch dishes I usually prefer to cook this keto kale gratin and taste it hot. I place all the ingredients early in the morning and let my Crock

Pot work a little. I have a super tender gratin for the lunch!

Ingredients (11 servings):

whole milk	1 cup
mascarpone	1/4 cup
unsalted butter	1 tablespoon
kale	1 to 2 medium
coconut flour	1/2 cup
salt	1/2 teaspoon
pepper	1 teaspoon
dried thyme	1 teaspoon
garlic powder	1 teaspoon
vegetable broth	1 cup
shredded gruyere	1 cup

Fresh parsley at will

Fresh chives if desired

Directions:
1. Shred the cheese and set aside.
2. Take a small bowl, whisk together mascarpone with milk.
3. Melt the butter in a saucepan.

4. Add chopped kale, flour, salt, pepper at will, thyme and garlic powder. Mix everything in a bowl. Add butter melted.
5. Pour in milk with mascarpone mixture, add the vegetable broth.
6. Add shredded gruyere. Mix well everything.
7. Pour the mix into the Crock Pot and set on HIGH for 3 hours.
8. Serve with fresh chopped parsley at will and chives if desired.
9. Bon Appetite!

Artichokes with Lemon Tarragon Dipping Sauce

My magic Crock Pot always controls my keto diet as well as allows me more time for my family. All its functions allow preparing incredible dishes combining uncommon products getting amazing eating qualities! You don't need to spend too much time in the kitchen to prepare lunch or dinner. If you eat artichokes with pleasure, everything you need is two small lemons, broth, and some species, like salt, tarragon, and pepper if you wish. Following my instructions, you could make two things at the same time – prepare the quick lunch that is beyond compare and spend the remaining time with family members.

Ingredients (7 servings):

Artichokes   4 pcs

Lemons	2 pcs
poultry broth	2 cups
tarragon	1 tablespoon
celery	1 stalk
olive oil	1/2 cup
sea salt	1/4 teaspoon

black pepper at will

Directions:
1. Cut the stalk of artichokes, they must be the one-inch length. Trim off one inch of the «petals». Chop the stalks, petal tips.
2. Peel the lemon zest. Slice it into four pieces, remove the seeds.
3. Chop finely the tarragon leaves.
4. Put lemon slices to the bottom of the Crock Pot, top each piece with artichokes, pour the bone broth around the artichokes.
5. Cover and cook on LOW for 1-2 hours.
6. At the time while artichokes are cooking, prepare the dipping sauce. Chop the tarragon leaves, chop celery into small pieces. Throw the seeds from the remained lemon, chop it finely.
7. Put the lemon slices, zest, tarragon leaves, olive oil, celery, salt to the blender or a food processor. Blend until smooth texture.

8. Once the cooking time of artichokes is over, serve them topped with prepared sauce.
9. Enjoy your lunch time!

Keto Spicy Broccoli Stems

You may wonder, what I'm cooking today as a side dish. Yes, this dish is always on the list of non-appreciated veggies and don't get a huge respect for the majority of people. Usually, people don't save the broccoli stems – it is like a rubbish. But! Wait. It could be served as a side dish too! Why not!? I used to eat the broccoli stems in salads. As I have gathered a large package of broccoli stems I decided to cook them finally! You may use any variations of them – combine the stems with Feta or another kind of cheese, add the preferred sauce or topping, dress with black pepper, cilantro and lime! I realized that I could eat this spicy broccoli stems like a main dish. Here is my recipe!

Ingredients (8 servings):

broccoli stems	1 lb. (ca. 8 thick stems)
oil (avocado or olive)	1 tablespoon
minced garlic	1 tablespoon
green onion for garnish (optional)	1/4 cup

Sauce Ingredients:

soy sauce (low sodium)	1 tablespoon

Hoisin sauce	2 teaspoon
Chili Garlic Sauce	2 teaspoon
Splenda or Stevia	1 tablespoon

Pepper and salt at will

Directions:

Wash the broccoli stems, this time you have to trim away all discolored parts. Using a sharp knife, trim away the extra leaves, ribs from stems. Take a vegetable peeler and peel them. Cut the ready-prepared stems into slices (cut diagonal), ca. ½-inch thick.

1. Take a medium bowl and mix soy sauce, chili garlic sauce, Hoisin sauce, sweetener. Peel the garlic, mince it and add to the mixture.
2. Whisk everything well. Slice thinly green onions.
3. Spray the oil over the bottom of the Crock Pot, place the stems, pour the sauce over the stems. Stir well everything.
4. Cover and put on HIGH for 1 hours. Stir from time to time the stems.
5. Check the broccoli stems, don't let them burn. They must get a little crisp.
6. Serve hot, dress with the rest of green onions, black pepper and salt at will.
7. Bon Appetite!

Chapter 3: Desserts Recipes

Keto Crock Pot Quick Cake

The ingredients for this quick cake are rather simple, moreover, you can use already prepared at the store chocolate chips. Remember only, they must be sugar-free. This recipe of the quick keto cake is great to prepare when the guests are coming and you still don't have something tasty.

Ingredients (8 servings):

Butter	1 tablespoon
almond flour	3 tablespoon
sweetener	1 tablespoon
cinnamon	1 pinch
yolk	1 egg
vanilla extract	1/8 teaspoon
salt	1 pinch

sugar-free chocolate chips 2 tablespoon

Directions:
1. Melt butter in a medium-sized pan, let it brown a little.
2. Mix the browned butter with the mentioned amount of almond flour in a bowl.
3. Add sweetener and cinnamon. Mix everything well.
4. Add the egg yolk, after this add vanilla extract, a pinch of salt.
5. Add the sugar-free chocolate chips. Stir to combine.
6. Open the Crock Pot and spray a surface and sides with cooking spray or oil and place your mixture.
7. Close the Crock Pot and put on high for an hour.
8. Once the time is over, let it cool some minutes and then dig in!
9. Enjoy with ice cream.
10. Bon Appetite!

Almond Butter Fudge Bars

Almond fudge bars is a great recipe to make with the whole members of your family. One can enjoy the bars as a quick snack, breakfast, lunch-time, or night dessert)) Homemade desserts are always better than bought at the storage. The Almond Butter Fudge Bars, I advise you to bake, have a crispy crust and are great with heavy-creamy or some toppings.

Ingredients (9 servings):

almond flour	1 cup
unsalted butter	1/2 cup
powdered erythritol (sweetener)	6 tablespoons
ground cinnamon	1/2 teaspoon
heavy cream	1/4 cup
almond butter	1/2 cup
vanilla extract	1/2 teaspoon
xanthan gum	1/8 teaspoon

80% dark chocolate or sugar-free chocolate chips
1 ounce

Directions:
1. Open the Crock Pot and spread the cooking spray over the sides and the bottom.
2. Melt the butter and divide into portions.
3. In a medium-sized bowl whisk together almond flour, melted butter, powdered erythritol, cinnamon. Combine everything well.
4. Spread the mixture on the bottom of the Crock-Pot, cover and set on HIGH for one hour. The mixture must get golden brown.
5. Take off the almond base and let it cool. Chop the dark chocolate finely.

6. Whisk together in a large bowl heavy cream with almond butter, remained butter and powdered erythritol.
7. Add the vanilla and xanthan gum and blend everything well.
8. Spread the mixture over the cooled almond base and sprinkle with chopped dark chocolate or if desired with chocolate chips.
9. Freeze overnight, slice the base into bars and serve.
10. Enjoy!

Chewy Ginger Cake Crock Pot

My Chewy Ginger Cake is made with erythritol that allows for our keto rules. I usually bake this cake for holidays and weekends. It is great making in the Crock Pot, simple and tasty. Why not trying to prepare?

Ingredients:

almond flour	1.5 cups
coconut flour	3/4 cup
ground ginger	1/2 tablespoon
ground cinnamon	1 teaspoon
sea salt	1/4 teaspoon
unsalted butter	3/4 cup
powdered erythritol	3/4 cup

eggs	1 large

Directions:

1. Open the Crock Pot and spread the cooking spray over the sides and the bottom.
2. Whisk in a medium-sized bowl almond flour, coconut flour, cinnamon, ginger, and salt.
3. Take another medium bowl, combine together butter with erythritol until fluffy and light.
4. Crack the egg and slowly beat it in the dry mixture.
5. Turn out the dough ball knead until it comes everything together. Scoop into a ball.
6. Roll the dough ball in powdered erythritol, place it into the bottom of the Crock Pot.
7. Put on LOW for 2-3 hours and bake until golden brown.
8. Bon Appetite!

Halloween Mud Pie Keto Recipe

Trick or Treat... Or both? When the Halloween is around the corner you must bake this pie definitely! Yes, it takes you some time to prepare this tasty one. If you can find sugar-free gummy worms in the store, feel free to prepare them.

Ingredients (18 servings):
Sugar-Free Gummy Worms:

sugar-free Jell-O (8 grams each)	2 packets
gelatin (8 grams)	2 packets

water	1/2 cup

Cake Base:

almond flour	2 cups
coconut flour	2 tablespoon
cocoa powder	1/2 cup
erythritol	1 cup
baking soda	1.5 teaspoon
salt	1/2 teaspoon
butter (melted)	1 cup
eggs	3 large
vanilla extract	2 teaspoon
heavy cream	1/2 cup
almond milk	1/4 cup

Frosting:

Butter	1/4 cup
cocoa powder	1.5 tablespoon
powdered erythritol	1/2 cup
almond milk	2 tablespoon

Directions:

1. Begin to prepare the sugar-free gummy worms: put a small pot on low heat, whisk together sugar-free Jell-O, gelatin and a cup water.
2. Once all the clumps of gelatin are done, pour the ready-made liquid into the gummy molds. Refrigerate them overnight.

Baking the base:

1. Open the Crock Pot and spread the cooking spray over the sides and the bottom.
2. Whisk together all the dry ingredients in a medium-sized bowl - almond flour, coconut flour, baking soda, salt, erythritol.
3. Melt the butter.
4. Add also the wet ingredients - butter, cracked eggs, vanilla extract, heavy cream, almond milk.
5. Open the Crock Pot and spread the cooking spray over the sides and the bottom.
6. Pour the batter into the Crock Pot, cover and set on LOW for 4 hours.
7. Once the time is over, let it cool completely.
8. Prepare the frosting that will hold the end result together: take a saucepan and melt the butter.
9. Turn off the heat, stir in the cocoa powder, erythritol, almond milk. Whisk everything until smooth.
10. Once the cake is cooled, put it in a large mixing bowl and crumble it completely with your hands, pour the frosting, mix everything again.

11. Put (press) in the gummy worms you have made already. Make sure to press them firmly.
12. Once you get to the top layer, press everything good. Add the last part of the gummy worms to the top, being as creative as you like. Add some sugar-free chocolate chips to the cake top.
13. Enjoy and Happy Halloween!

Pumpkin Pie Keto Fat Bomb

Never heard about pumpkin pie keto fat bomb? Pure you! I decided to use the coconut butter in this recipe and I must tell you it is great and must get enough attention by preparing the desserts. It tastes like coconut, has a texture of peanut butter and is great for preparing cakes. It is ideal for keto diet and my family like it very much!

Ingredients (7 servings):

pumpkin puree	1/2 cup
coconut butter	2 oz.
coconut oil	1/2 cup
sweetener	1/4 cup
pumpkin pie spice	2 teaspoon
cup pecans	½
almond flour	1 cup

Directions:

1. Melt the coconut oil if it's not already liquid.
2. In a medium-sized saucepan melt the coconut butter until softened.
3. Combine in a mixing bowl the pumpkin puree, coconut butter, and coconut oil and stir everything well.
4. Add the sweetener.
5. Add the pumpkin pie spice as well. If you don't have it, just add cinnamon! Add flour.
6. Once your fat bomb is combined, pour this into the Crock Pot. Don't forget the spread the bottom and the sides of the Crock Pot with cooking spray!
7. Toast up chopped pecans a little in a dry pan until slightly browned and fragrant.
8. Add the pecans to the mixture.
9. Cover the Crock Pot and set on LOW for 2 -3 hours.
10. Enjoy warm!
11. Bon Appetite!

White Chocolate Green Tea Mug Keto Cake

Green tea mug keto cake is one of my lovely and unusual cakes ever. Firstly, I tried it in the restaurant, its colored has surprised me at once! But what an amazing taste it has! I cooked it at home and found it was nothing difficult to prepare. The only necessary ingredient you have to put there is matcha powder. This ingredient makes the dessert flavorful, decadent, rich and funny!

Ingredients (11 servings):

powdered erythritol	1.5 tablespoon
liquid stevia	5-10 drops
egg	1 large
coconut oil (or melted butter)	1 tablespoon
vanilla extract	1/2 teaspoon
almond flour	1/4 cup
matcha powder	1/2 teaspoon
baking powder	1 teaspoon
xanthan gum	1/8 teaspoon
sea salt	1 pinch
frozen sugar-free white chocolate chips	2 tablespoon

Directions:
1. Freeze the sugar-free white chocolate chips beforehand to ensure they stay as chips while baking.
2. Open the Crock Pot and spread the cooking spray over the sides and the bottom.
3. Take a large bowl, whisk the erythritol and stevia into the egg.

4. Add the coconut oil (or if you use the butter - melted butter) and vanilla extract and whisk everything well to combine.
5. In another medium-sized bowl combine together almond flour, matcha powder, baking powder and xanthan gum.
6. Add this mix to the other wet ingredients. Add also a pinch salt, combine everything very well.
7. Fold in the white chocolate chips.
8. Pour in the Crock Pot, cover and set on LOW for 2 hours.
9. Once the baking time is over, let the cake cool and enjoy!
10. Bon Appetite!

Keto Peanut Butter Cake

Peanut butter cake has a special place among my keto desserts prepared in the Crock Pot. There are only three ingredients needed for the cake. They are the sweetener, peanut butter, and a fresh egg. It is simple enough, even kids can prepare this delicious cake.

Ingredients (3 servings):

peanut butter	1 cup
granular erythritol	1/2 cup
egg	1 large

Directions:
1. Open the Crock Pot and spread the cooking spray over the sides and the bottom.
2. Blend a half of an amount of granular erythritol into a food processor and blend for some seconds. You should get a finely powdered sweetener.
3. In a medium-sized bowl combine peanut butter with powdered erythritol and the fresh egg, mix everything well.
4. Roll the cake into a medium-sized ball and place on a bottom of the Crock Pot.
5. Cover the Crock Pot and set on LOW for 3 hours. Check the readiness from time to time, the cake edges must turn a darker brown.
6. Once the baking time is over, take off the cake and let it cool.
7. Enjoy with a glass of milk!

Black and White Keto Cake

An amazing keto cake that consists of chocolate and… chocolate! White and black! Always more chocolate for chocolate fans! Yes, I'm sure, you will not forget this texture! Don't forget to use sugar-free and keto-friendly ingredients in this recipe! It is a perfect alternative to sweets and chocolate!

Ingredients (16 servings):
For Cake

Almond flour	2 cups

coconut flour	2 tablespoon
sweetener	1 cup
baking soda	1.5 teaspoon
salt	1/2 teaspoon
butter	1 cup
cocoa powder	1/2 cup
water	1 cup
eggs	3 large
vanilla extract	2 tsp
sour cream	1/2 cup

White Chocolate Glaze:

Cocoa Butter Wafers	2 oz.
powdered erythritol	3 tablespoon
vanilla extract	1 teaspoon
heavy cream	2 tablespoon

Topping

Cocoa Nibs	20 grams

Directions:
1. Open the Crock Pot and spread the cooking spray over the sides and the bottom.

2. In a medium-sized bowl whisk together almond flour with coconut flour, sweetener baking soda, and salt. Set aside.
3. Take a small pot, heat together butter, cocoa powder, water on a high heat. Whisk everything until combined and take it off from the heat.
4. Pour a half of chocolate mixture into dry ingredients (first bowl) and stir to combine. Once the mixture is thick and difficult to stir, pour the other half. Combine once more.
5. Add in 1 egg, after this add sour cream and vanilla extract, stir everything well.
6. Pour the batter into the Crock Pot and set on LOW for 5 hours, until the wooden toothpick comes out clean.
7. While the cake is baking, it is time to prepare white chocolate glaze.
8. In a little saucepan melt cocoa butter wafers.
9. Add powdered erythritol and mix to combine.
10. Add heavy cream and put the mixture in the fridge, stirring every 6-7 minutes.
11. Once the chocolate has chilled to the thick consistency, pulse it for some seconds in a blender until smooth.
12. Once the cake is ready, let it cool for about 10 minutes, then put it on a plate and let it cool completely.
13. After this glaze the cake. Let the glaze drape over the top of the cake.
14. Dress with the nibs.
15. Enjoy!

Keto Pumpkin Cake

Keto pumpkin cake prepared in the Crock Pot is great for everyday desserts. It is delicious creamy pumpkin base with a coffee cake crumble flavor topping. I'm sure, it will magically disappear from the kitchen once it is ready!

Ingredients (16 servings):

coconut flour	1/3 cup
pumpkin pie spice	2 teaspoon
cinnamon	1 teaspoon
salt	1/8 teaspoon
eggs	2 pcs
organic pumpkin puree	1/3 cup
sweetener	1/3 cup
coconut milk	1/4 cup
coconut oil	2 tablespoon
vanilla extract	1 teaspoon
baking soda	½ teaspoon

Crumble Topping:

pecan meal	1/2 cup
coconut flakes	3 tablespoon

coconut sugar	2 tablespoon
cinnamon	1 teaspoon
coconut oil	3 tablespoon

Directions:

1. Open the Crock Pot and spread the cooking spray over the sides and the bottom.
2. Take a medium-sized mixing bowl and combine coconut flour, pumpkin pie spice, cinnamon, and sea salt. Mix everything thoroughly. Set aside.
3. Take another large mixing bowl and combine eggs, coconut milk, pumpkin puree, melted coconut oil or butter, sweetener, and vanilla extract. Mix together until combined.
4. Add baking soda to the egg mixture. Mix together thoroughly.
5. Add coconut flour mix to the egg mix and stir until combined.
6. Pour into the Crock Pot and set aside.
7. In a little bowl combine pecan meal, coconut flakes, coconut sugar, oil, and cinnamon, use a fork to mix until paste forms.
8. Take the crumble topping all over the top of the pumpkin batter in the Crock Pot.
9. Cover the Crock Pot and set on LOW for 4 hours until top is browned, and a toothpick comes out clean.

10. Cool the cake completely, then refrigerate for one hour or longer.
11. Bon Appetite!

Keto Pumpkin Chocolate Chip

This dessert recipe is something special because of the mix sweet coconut flour, chocolate chips with cardamom, ginger powder and ground cloves. But be sure, it rather tasty, flavor and simple.

Ingredients (13 servings):

almond butter unsweetened	1/2 cup
pumpkin puree unsweetened	1/4 cup
erythritol granulated	1/4 cup
ginger powder	1/4 teaspoon
nutmeg	1/4 teaspoon
cardamon powder	1/4 teaspoon
ground cloves	1/4 teaspoon
cinnamon	1 teaspoon
stevia powder	1/4 teaspoon
baking soda	1/2 teaspoon
coconut flour	1 tablespoon
chocolate chips	2 tablespoon

egg	1pcs

Directions:
1. Open the Crock Pot and spread the cooking spray over the sides and the bottom.
2. Mix in a large bowl pumpkin puree, almond butter, sweetener, ginger powder, nutmeg, cardamom powder, freshly cracked egg, ground cloves, cinnamon, stevia powder, baking soda, coconut flour. Stir everything well.
3. Add chocolate chips.
4. Put the mixture into the Crock Pot, cover and set on HIGH for 2 hours.
5. Take out and let it cool.
6. Bon Appetite!

Keto Crock Pot Cheesecake

When I tried to cook this recipe for the first time I couldn't believe the cheesecake could be so easy!!!! It is amazing, flavor and tender cake! I think I don't need to tell you more about the cheesecake. You may serve it with low carb fruit sauce, berries. The best way – to let it cool in the refrigerator for a night, but I can't stand it!

Ingredients (4 servings):

cream cheese	3 8 oz. packages
eggs	3 pcs
Splenda	1 cup

Vanilla   ½ tablespoon

Directions:
1. Let the cheese (cream cheese) get the room temperature. Place it in a medium-sized bowl, add Splenda.
2. Using a blender mix everything well, until cheese and Splenda are blended thoroughly.
3. Add the cracked eggs, one after one blending all the time the mixture.
4. Spray the bottom and the sides of the Crock Pot with cooking spray, pour the egg-cheese mixture into the Crock Pot.
5. Cover and put the dish on HIGH for 2 hours.
6. Look after an hour from time to time. Check the readiness of the cheesecake – the knife must go out from the cake clean.
7. Let it cool.
8. Bon Appetite!

Keto Crock Pot Pumpkin Custard

This pumpkin custard is one of my favorite because it is baked in the Crock Pot. It is very flavorful and creamy. I just mix all the ingredients in a large bowl, blend well and after this pour to the Crock Pot. I usually use Stevia in my recipes (blended variation) or you may use another sweetener if you want. Instead of the vanilla extract, you may use the maple syrup if you like.

Ingredients (8 servings):

Eggs	4 large
granulated stevia	1/2 cup
pumpkin puree (canned)	1 cup
vanilla extract	1 teaspoon
superfine almond flour	1/2 cup
pumpkin pie spice	1 teaspoon
sea salt	1/8 teaspoon
butter, ghee	4 tablespoons

Directions:
1. Blend the granulated Stevia. Set aside.
2. Break the eggs into a bowl, compound them until smooth consistency (the mix must thicken slightly). Add a little bit the vanilla extract, put the pumpkin puree. Combine everything well once more.
3. Add slowly pie spice, salt, flour and stir thoroughly. Go on the blend.
4. Melt butter or ghee, pour slowly into the blended mixture. Stir everything well.
5. Spray the cooking spray over the bottom of the Crock Pot, pour the compound into the Crock Pot.
6. Put the paper towel over the top of the Crock Pot, a cap must be covered. So, it means the

towel is arranged between the cap and the top. It must absorb the condensed damp.

7. Put the Crock Pot on LOW for ca. 3 hours. Check from time to time. When the dish is ready, the sides must put off from the Crock Pot.
8. Take off the custard from the Crock Pot, serve with Stevia whipped cream and nutmeg at will.
9. Bon Appetite!

Lemon Crock Pot Cake

This amazing lemon keto cake was prepared during 3 hours without any strong efforts. I must say, this keto cake tasted better the next day as it was kept all the night in the refrigerator. I think the cakes made of coconut or almond flour taste better when you keep them at least some hours in the refrigerator.

Ingredients:
Baking a cake:

almond flour	1 1/2 cup
coconut flour	1/2 cup
Puree all-purpose (or Swerve)	3 teaspoons
baking powder	2 teaspoons
xanthan gum optional	1/2 teaspoon
butter melted	1/2 cup

whipping cream	1/2 cup
Juice of lemon	2 tablespoons
Zest from two lemons	
Eggs	2 pcs

Cooking a topping:

Puree all-purpose (or Swerve)	3 teaspoons
baking powder	2 teaspoons
boiling water	1/2 cup
butter melted	2 tablespoons
lemon juice	2 tablespoons

Directions:
Baking a cake:

1. Take a medium-sized bowl, conjoin the coconut flour, sweetener, almond flour, baking powder, xanthan gum. Stir well everything
2. In another bowl whisk the butter, squeeze the lemon juice, xanthan gum, whipping cream, zest, crack the egg in a bowl.
3. Combine both mixtures dry and wet one.
4. Spray the cooking spray over the Crock Pot, pour the mixture into the Crock Pot. Cover and put on HIGH for 3 hours until the inserted in the center knife comes out clean.

5. While the cake is cooking, prepare the topping – conjoin the baking powder, water, melted butter and lemon juice.
6. Take off the cake once it is ready for a large plate. Pour the topping over it.
7. Add whipped cream or fresh fruits by serving, if desired.
8. Bon Appetite!

Keto Chocolate Cake

This should be definitely the best low carb cake recipe one has ever tried to cook and to eat! It is reach and flavor! I guess, it is no need to describe the chocolate cake prepared in the Crock Pot. It is delicious. Just cook it following the directions below.

Ingredients (10 servings):

almond flour	1 cup and additionally 2 tablespoon
sweetener	1/2 cup
cocoa powder	1/2 cup
whey protein powder	3 tablespoon
baking powder	1 1/2 teaspoon
salt	1/4 teaspoon
eggs	3 large pcs
butter melted	6 tablespoon

unsweetened almond milk 2/3 cup

vanilla extract   3/4 teaspoon

Directions:
1. Spray the bottom and all the sides of the Crock Pot with cooking spray.
2. Take a bowl, mix well the almond flour, cocoa powder, sweetener, protein powder, baking powder, salt. Stir everything well.
3. Add butter (melted), cracked eggs, milk, vanilla. Combine everything.
4. Pour the ready-made mixture into the Crock Pot, cover and put on LOW for ca. 2 hours. It must look like a pudding.
5. Take off from the Crock Pot and let it cool.
6. Serve warm with whipping cream.
7. Bon Appetite!

Crock Pot Raspberry-Vanilla Pudding Cake

If you have a small container of fresh raspberries, don't hesitate to cook this amazing cake! It is a flavor, appetizing, tender pudding cake. The mixture is rather simple, it contains egg-free texture with an addition of boiling hot water at the end of cooking process. This dessert is amazing, keto-friendly, simple. Top this cake with vanilla, fresh raspberries and whipping cream.

Ingredients (10 servings):

Sweetener	2 cups
almond flour	2 cups
baking powder	4 teaspoon
salt	1 teaspoon
milk	1 cup
butter	4 tablespoon
vanilla	1 teaspoon
fresh raspberries	2 (6 oz) container
vanilla pudding mix	1 tablespoon
boiling water	1 3/4 cup

some fresh raspberries for dressing

Vanilla or whipped cream

Directions:
1. Take a medium bowl, combine flour, sweetener, baking powder, vanilla, salt, milk. Whisk everything. Melt the butter and add to the mixture.
2. Open the container with raspberries and pour them into the mixture.
3. Spread the cooking spray over the sides and bottom of the Crock Pot.

4. Put the mixture into the Crock Pot and spread it on the bottom.
5. Sprinkle the pudding mix over the top of the mixture but don't stir it.
6. Take a little bowl, let the water boil.
7. Pour the water carefully over the top of the pudding mix and the mixture.
8. Cover and put on HIGH for 2 hours.
9. The ready-made pudding will be on the bottom of the cake.
10. Serve with whipping cream or vanilla and fresh raspberries.
11. Bon Appetite!

Crock Pot Mocha Pudding Cake

This dessert cooked in the Crock Pot is something between a pudding and a chocolate cake. It has a tender, velvety texture, the chocolate and coffee notes give this dessert an amazing mocha taste! It doesn't need too much time, everything is rather simple. I would say, this cake could be cooked even by beginners!

Ingredients (10 servings):

Butter	¾ cup
unsweetened chocolate	2 ounces
heavy cream	½ cup
instant coffee crystals	2 tablespoons

vanilla extract	1 teaspoon
cocoa powder	4 tablespoons
almond flour	1/3 cup
salt	1/8 teaspoon
eggs	5 large pcs
Stevia	2/3 cup

coconut oil spray for the sides and bottom of the Crock Pot

Optional: whipped cream for serving

Directions:
1. Cut butter into large chunks.
2. Chop finely unsweetened chocolate.
3. Spray the bottom of the Crock Pot with cooking spray.
4. Take a little bowl, melt butter together with unsweetened chocolate. Whisk it all the time, don't let it burn. Set aside and let it cool.
5. Take another medium bowl, whisk coffee crystals, heavy cream, vanilla extract.
6. Take one more bowl and combine the cocoa, salt, almond flour. Stir well.
7. Using a mixer or a blender, whisk the eggs on a high speed until thickened slightly. Add sweetener.
8. Turn the speed of the mixer (or blender) on low, pour the butter with chocolate. Continue mixing.

9. Stir almond flour, salt and cocoa mixture too.
10. Add also to the blending mixture coffee, cream and vanilla mix.
11. Pour the compound into the Crock Pot. Put a paper (towel) over the Crock Pot and cover with cap.
12. Put on LOW for 3 hours.
13. Check the readiness of the cake – the edges must be like a cake, the center – must have a soft consistency.
14. Serve the cake with whipped cream if desired.
15. Bon Appetite!

Keto Black Raspberry Cheesecake

Do you prefer raspberries? Do you like cheesecake? If yes – this amazing flavor combination is definitely for you! I have combined the best ingredients I had in my refrigerator. It is very simple, keto cake you must try! I promise you will not be upset!

Ingredients (8 servings):

black raspberries (fresh) possible)	1 pint (frozen are also
lemon juice	2 tablespoon
cream cheese softened	16 ounces
Greek-style yogurt	6 ounces
vanilla extract	2 teaspoon

liquid stevia	25 drops
eggs	2 pcs
black raspberries, for garnish	½ cup

Directions:

1. Tale a medium-sized skillet and put over medium heat, place the raspberries. Stir them frequently. They must reduce the jam. It takes about 15 minutes.
2. Use a potato masher, break the raspberries up. Any pieces must remain.
3. Add lemon juice and let the mixture cool.
4. Take a large bowl combine liquid stevia and cream cheese, Greek yogurt, vanilla. Using a blender mix everything well, until the ingredients are blended thoroughly.
5. Add the cracked eggs, one after one blending all the time the mixture.
6. Spray the bottom and the sides of the Crock Pot with cooking spray, pour the egg-cheese mixture into the Crock Pot.
7. Cover and put the dish on HIGH for 2 hours.
8. Check the readiness of the cheesecake – the knife must go out from the cake clean.
9. Take off the cake from the Crock Pot and pour the raspberry on top. Dress with fresh raspberries.
10. Place in the refrigerator for 2 hours.
11. Bon Appetite!

Crock Pot Blueberry Lemon Custard Cake

Today I recommend you to cook very tasty lemon-blueberries custard cake. It is a light amazing combination of berries and creamy lemon. I like the recipes especially desserts, prepared with coconut flour as it gets delicious and moist. Garnish this perfect dessert with light cream or fresh blueberries!

Ingredients (9 servings):

Eggs	6 pcs
Coconut Flour	1/2 cup
lemon zest	2 teaspoons
lemon juice	1/3 cup
lemon liquid Stevia	1 teaspoon
Swerve sweetener	1/2 cup
Salt	1/2 teaspoon
light cream	2 cups
fresh blueberries	1/2 cup

lemon slices and fresh blueberries for garnish

Directions:
1. Break the eggs into a bowl, compound them until smooth consistency (the mix must thicken

slightly). Add Swerve sweetener and salt. Combine everything well once more.

2. Add flour and stir thoroughly. Go on the blend.
3. Mix the lemon zest, juice, and liquid Stevia, blueberries, stir well everything.
4. Spray the cooking spray over the bottom of the Crock Pot, pour the compound into the Crock Pot.
5. Put the paper towel over the top of the Crock Pot, cover with lid. The paper towel must absorb the condensed damp.
6. Put the Crock Pot on LOW for ca. 3 hours.
7. Take off the custard from the Crock Pot, serve with fresh blueberries, lemon slices, and light cream at will.
8. Bon Appetite!

Crock Pot Keto Crème Brulee

To prepare this amazing crème Brulee needs only 4 simple servings and 2-3 hours in the Crock Pot. The preparation process, I mean making some circles of foil, seems a little bit difficult than just to put the mixture to the Crock Pot at once. But in no way, it is not so difficult as you think. Just follow the directions and enjoy!

Ingredients (4 servings):

egg yolks   3 large

heavy whipping cream   1/2 cup

| Sweetener | 1/4 cup plus 2 teaspoons |
| vanilla bean | 1/4 pcs |

(or vanilla extract – 1 teaspoon)

Directions:
1. Take a medium saucepan, mix the egg yolks, 1/4 cup of Sweetener, whipping cream. Stir everything well.
2. With helping of a special dull knife, try to take off the seeds from the bean. Add them to the mixture. Once you couldn't scrape out the seeds, use the vanilla extract and add it also to the crème mixture.
3. Take medium-sized pieces (about 2 12") of foil, make a so-called «snake shape» rolling them up. Make it in a circle, pinch the ends together. Put this circle into the bottom of the Crock Pot, do the same with next piece.
4. Put each ramekin on a top of the circle of foil.
5. Let the water boil in a little bowl, pour it. Be careful! The water must reach about 1/3 of the way on ramekins.
6. Put the Crock Pot on LOW for 2,5 -max. 3 hours. Check the custard once the time is over.
7. Chill custard for 5 hours.
8. Before serving spread the remained sweetener over the custard.
9. Bon Appetite!

Crock Pot Keto Cinnamon Almonds

The keto cinnamon almonds are super both as dessert and as an appetizing. It makes amazing smell all over your house! The cinnamon almonds are the favorite keto-dish of all my family.

Ingredients (7 servings):

Sweetener	1 cup
Cinnamon	3 tablespoon
Salt	⅛ teaspoon
Egg White	⅛ teaspoon
Vanilla	2 teaspoon
Almonds	3 Cups
Water	⅛ Cups

Directions:

1. Take a bowl, conjoin sweetener, salt, cinnamon.
2. Take another one bowl, whisk thoroughly the egg white, vanilla. Place almonds and toss thoroughly. The cooking procedure let the sweet mix stick to almonds.
3. Spread the spray over the Crock Pot, put the cinnamon mixture with almonds, put it to LOW. Toss until the mix cover well all the almonds.
4. Cook ca. 3 hours. Stir all the time every 15 minutes. Add a little bit water and stir well.

5. Remove the almonds from the Crock Pot to the baking sheet, spread them and let them cool. Separate them from one another.
6. Enjoy!

Keto Lemon Coconut Cake With Cream Cheese Icing

The base of this keto Crock Pot cake is flavor, tender and delicious! I can't describe it with words, this is amazing and appetizing! The icing on this cake cooked with cream cheese, lemon zest, and vanilla is a perfectly integral addition to the cake!

Ingredients (12 servings):
Coconut Cake:

Coconut Flour	1/2 Cup
Eggs	5 pcs
Erythritol	1/4 Cup
Butter Melted	1/2 Cup
Lemon Juiced	½ teaspoon
Lemon Zest	1/2 teaspoon
xanthan gum	1/2 teaspoon
Salt	1/2 teaspoon

Icing:

Cream Cheese	1 Cup
Natvia	3 tablespoons
Vanilla Extract	1 teaspoon
Lemon Zest	½ teaspoon

Directions:

1. Firstly, separate the yolks and whites of eggs. Whisk the whites until smooth in a large bowl.
2. Place the coconut flour, juice of lemon, zest, xanthan gum, salt in the same bowl. Melt the butter and pour also. Continue whisking.
3. Spread the cooking spray over the Crock Pot (bottom and sides), pour the mixture into it.
4. Cover and put on LOW for 3 hours.
5. While the cake is cooking, take a little bowl, whisk there Natvia, cream cheese, vanilla, zest together with a blender.
6. Once the cake is ready, remove it to a plate and top with the icing.
7. Bon Appetite!

Crock Pot Keto Coffee Cake

This recipe is for those who like coffee most of all. I think you will definitely like this brown, tender cake. It is amazing, delicious, flavor cake. The syrup will be a great addition to the ready-made cake!

Ingredients (10 servings):

| sour cream | 1/2 cup |

coffee	1/3 cup
softened butter	½ cup
eggs	3 pcs
sugar substitute (Swerve)	1/2 cup
almond flour	2 1/4 cup
baking powder	2 1/2 teaspoon

Syrup:

Water	1/3 cup
sweetener	1/3 cup
instant coffee	1/2 teaspoon

Directions:
1. Take a medium bowl, conjoin the sour cream, coffee, until smooth. Add softened butter, stir well. Mix everything until smooth. Add the eggs, whisk all the time.
2. Stir the sweetener.
3. Take another bowl, conjoin baking powder and almond flour. Put this mixture into the coffee mix.
4. After you have combined all the mixtures, pour this into the Crock Pot covered with cooking spray.
5. Cover and cook on LOW for 2-3 hours.
6. Check with a toothpick if the cake is ready.

7. Prepare the syrup – mix the water and Swerve on a medium heat. Whisk until all the ingredients are dissolved. Pour the instant coffee. Let it cool a little.
8. Once the cake is ready, remove it to the plate, pour the syrup over it.
9. Cut and enjoy!
10. Bon Appetite!

Crock Pot Angel Food Cake

The Angel food cake is light like a cloud or a fresh air! The cream of tartar that I have firstly used in this recipe stabilizes all the beaten egg whites that are of special importance in this recipe for the Crock Pot. I like to eat this cake with macerated berries and whipped cream because I think it is the best combination I could only imagine! You may also use the other berries of your keto diet you prefer more, but don't forget about forbidden and allowed products!

Ingredients (8 servings):

Sweetener	¾ cup
Almond flour	½ cup
Kosher salt	¼ teaspoon
Egg whites	5 large
Cream of tartar	½ teaspoon
Vanilla extract	1 teaspoon

Macerated Strawberries

Whipped cream

Strawberries for dressing

Directions:
1. Firmly wring a 3-foot length of foil (aluminum foil), after this shape it into a zigzag form width-wise the oval or round Crock Pot. Just try to create a rack, adding 1 cup of water.
2. Place the top of the Crock Pot and set on LOW after this.
3. Take a medium bowl, whisk together flour, sweetener, salt and set aside everything.
4. Take another little bowl, crack the eggs (whites) and add slowly tartar. Using the blender or the food processor, mix everything on a medium speed. It takes usually 1-2 minutes. You may increase the speed slowly until the texture gets foamy. Add vanilla.
5. Pour the mixture with sweetener from the first bowl into the second one, whisk all together.
6. Transfer the batter to a loaf pan and smooth top.
7. Place the loaf pan into the Crock Pot, press into the aluminum foil rack just to ensure the level of the pan. Take a clean kitchen towel and drape over the Crock Pot. Put the lead over it.
8. Put the Crock Pot on LOW approximately 2-3 hours. Once 1,5 hours is over start to check the readiness of the cake in the Crock Pot.

9. Once the cake is ready, remove the pan from the Crock Pot and let it cool about 20 minutes.
10. Using a knife, run it around the edges separating the ready cake from the pan.
11. Remove it to the serving plate.
12. Dress with macerated strawberries at will and the whipped cream.
13. Bon Appetite!

Crock Pot Milk Cake Low-Carb

I hope this recipe will be the real beginning for those who have never used his/her Crock Pot. This recipe for the delicious cake is definitely for you! The main option here, I think, it is that you don't need to sit all the time waiting for your cake and controlling the Crock Pot. That is what I exactly like my Crock Pot for!

Ingredients (8 servings):
For Cake

eggs	3 pcs fresh
Condensed Milk 14 oz	2 cans
Evaporated Milk substitute 14 oz (1 can)	
Almond Flour	2 1/2 cups
Butter softened	3 tablespoons
sweetener	1/4 cup

For Topping

Milk 14 oz	1 can
sweetener	2 tablespoons
vanilla extract	0,5 tablespoon

Directions:
For Cake

1. Take a large bowl and mix there cracked eggs whisked thoroughly, condensed milk, evaporated milk substitute, almond flour, butter softened, add sweetener. Stir everything well together.
2. Spray the cooking spray over the bottom and the sides of the Crock Pot, pour the mixture into the Crock Pot.
3. Put the paper towel on the top of the Crock Pot and put the Crock Pot on HIGH for 3 hours.

Prepare the topping:

1. Take a medium saucepan and mix sweetener, condensed milk, and vanilla let it boil until smooth texture.
2. Once the cake is ready, remove it from the Crock Pot on the plate and top with ready-made topping.
   Let the liquid absorb. You may serve it both warm or cool.
3. Bon Appetite!

Crock Pot Giant Chocolate Pie

A giant chocolate pie is a delicious, flavor recipe that is perfect for daily eating and for a party! You may also serve this pie with whipped cream. What is better – it is coking this pie in your Crock Pot that lets you mix all the ingredients and forget about cooking for some period of time. I'm sure, this chocolate pie recipe will be great adding for your supper or dinner!

Ingredients (8 servings):

butter at room temp	0,2 lb
sweetener	4 tablespoons
eggs	2 pcs fresh
vanilla extract	1 tablespoon
almond flour	0,4 lb
baking soda	1/2 teaspoon
salt	1/4 teaspoon

dark choc chips or dark chocolate low-carb
0,3 lb

Directions:
1. Take a middle bowl, mix together butter, sweetener, vanilla extract. Crack the fresh eggs. Whisk everything together.
2. Take another little bowl, conjoin flour, salt, and baking soda.

3. Stir the flour mixture into the mix of butter. You have to stir everything well until biscuit texture. The right consistency of the mixture means the sides of the bowl are clean.
4. Stir the choc chips and spread them thoroughly.
5. Spread the Crock Pot with the cooking spray, pour the mixture into the Crock Pot.
   Put the Crock Pot on LOW for 3 hours, it may also be needed to put the Crock Pot for 30 minutes on HIGH last 30 minutes.
6. Once the time is over, take off the pie from the Crock Pot and let it cool for 20 minutes.
7. Bon Appetite!

Keto Brownies Crock Pot

If you prefer the delicious combinations of peanut butter and chocolate chips low-carb, this one will be definitely for you! So easy to cook, so great to eat! For this recipe, you need only simple ingredients that could be bought at any market.

Ingredients (8 servings):

unsalted butter (melted)	½ cup
cocoa powder low-carb	2/3 cup
sweetener	1 1/3 cup
salt	1/2 teaspoon
eggs	2 pcs fresh

almond flour   3/4 cups

chocolate chips low-carb   2/3 cups

creamy peanut butter (melted)   1/3 cup

Directions:
1. Take a mixing bowl medium-sized, conjoin together melted butter, sweetener, cocoa, mix until smooth.
2. Add salt crack the fresh eggs, stir everything until incorporated.
3. Add the chocolate chips, distribute them thoroughly.
4. Spray the cooking spray over the Crock Pot bottom and sides, pour the batter into your Crock Pot.
5. Melt the peanut butter in a little pan, drizzle it over the brownie batter, swirl with a toothpick.
6. Add the remained chocolate chips over the brownie.
7. Cover the Crock Pot and cook on LOW for 2-2,5 hours mostly.
8. Once the time is over, open the Crock Pot and remove the cake.
9. Let it cool and enjoy!

Crock Pot Pumpkin Pecan Bread Pudding

I'm excited to present you today the pumpkin pecan bread pudding! I think it is high time to bake this delicious one. I hope you have already got a little bit experience and have already tried to cook the keto bread that's why it will be easy for you to perform this recipe. Have a little patience!

Ingredients (13 servings):

Keto bread cubes	8 cups
toasted pecans	1/2 cup
cinnamon chips	1/2 cup
eggs	4 pcs
canned pumpkin	1 cup
half n half	1 cup
sweetener	1/2 cup
butter melted	1/2 cup
vanilla	1 teaspoon
cinnamon	1/2 teaspoon
nutmeg	1/2 teaspoon
ginger	1/4 teaspoon
ground cloves	1/8 teaspoon

Vanilla ice cream if desired

Caramel ice cream topping at will

Directions:

1. Cut the bread slices into cubes. I remember you how to cook the keto bread – You have to take a medium bowl, mix butter and cream cheese. Stir until the creamy consistency. Add rosemary, sage, parsley to the mix and proceed to stir. Add cracked eggs and blend up to the smooth consistency.
Mix with baking powder, coconut and almond flour. Spray the Crock Pot with cooking spray. Pour the consistency to the Crock Pot. Cover and put on LOW 3-4 hours. Keto bread should be golden on top and come out clean. After the keto bread is done you may use the bread slices cut into cubes (use the old bread mostly).

2. Peel and shred the ginger. Peel the cloves. Chop the pecans.

3. Mix all together in a large bowl freshly cracked eggs, canned pumpkin, half-n-half, sweetener, melted butter, cinnamon, vanilla extract, nutmeg, ginger, and cloves.

4. Pour the mix on the top of the cubed bread. The mixture must coat the cubes gently.

5. Cover the Crock Pot and put it on LOW for 3,5 hours. Check until the toothpick inserts in the center and gently comes out clean.

6. Serve the bread pudding warm and top it with vanilla ice cream or if you prefer.

7. Bon Appetite!

Crock pot Cocoa Zucchini Bread

If you have some zucchinis at your refrigerator and you would like to cook something tasty, new and delicious – this unusual cocoa-zucchini bread is for you! After some hours (I mean actually two hours in the Crock Pot) you get a really new bread, flavorful and moist! I always put a little bit more cocoa chips than it is mentioned in the recipe because I like them very much, and I must say, it tastes even more wonderful! If you like to eat sweet bread, you may also put a little bit more sweetener. I hope you will try one day.

Ingredients (10 servings):

Eggs	3 pcs
Sweetener	1 1/2 cups
vegetable oil	1 cup
almond flour	3 cups
baking soda	1 teaspoon
cinnamon	2 teaspoon
vanilla	3 teaspoon
salt	1/4 teaspoon
cocoa chips low-carb	1 cup
zucchini	2 cups

Directions:
1. Wash the zucchini, peel and grate them. Set aside.
2. Take a medium-sized bowl, mix almond flour, baking soda, vanilla, cinnamon, salt. Combine everything well.
3. Take another little bowl, mix the sweetener, vegetable oil and cracked fresh eggs. Whisk together.
4. Join the shredded zucchini, cocoa chips and mix everything together from all the bowls. Stir well.
5. Spray the bottom and the sides of the Crock Pot with the cooking spray.
6. Pour the batter into the Crock Pot, cover and set on LOW for 3 hours.
7. Once the time is over, remove the cake to a plate and serve warm!
8. Bon Appetite!

Chocolate-Cinnamon Latte Cake

When we are speaking about the tasty and delicious cakes I always remember this recipe because I like coffee. This super easy Crock Pot recipe is based on a white cake mix that you have to prepare yourself following my instructions. It is easy and quick. Further, you add the ingredients listed below, pour the mixture into the Crock Pot (I recommend you to use the foil) and put on HIGH.

Serve the ready-made cake with ice cream or whipped cream.

Ingredients (12 servings):
For cake mix (homemade):

Almond flour	2 3/4 cup
Sweetener	1 3/4 cups
baking soda	2 teaspoon
salt	3/4 teaspoon

For cake:

unsweetened cocoa	1/3 cup
ground cinnamon	1/2 teaspoon
butter melted	1/2 cup
strong hot brewed coffee sugar-free	1 1/4 cups
eggs	3 large
evaporated milk unsweetened	1 (12-oz.) can
Vegetable cooking spray	
dark chocolate morsels package	1 (10-oz.)
whipped cream or coffee ice cream at will	

Directions:

1. Whisk together the ingredients for a cake mix in a medium-sized bowl (sweetener, almond flour, salt and baking soda).
2. Mix the previous ingredients with unsweetened cocoa, cinnamon, melted butter, coffee, cracked fresh eggs and unsweetened evaporated milk (substitute) in a large bowl. Stir everything well.
3. Spray with the cooking spray the bottom and the sides of the Crock Pot.
4. You may use the aluminum foil, allowing 2-3 inches to extend over the sides. Don't forget to grease the aluminum foil with cooking spray also. Pour the mixture into the Crock Pot and cover it. Cook on HIGH 1 ½ hours maximum.
5. Remove the lid and let it cool for 30 minutes.
6. Remove the cake from Crock Pot on a plate (use the foil sides as handles).
7. Serve warm or cool with whipped cream if desired or ice cream.
8. Bon Appetite!

Berry Cobbler Crock Pot

Summer is the time of easy and delicious cake recipes full of vitamins. Today I would like to bake the cobbler in my Crock Pot. I would like to use blueberries, raspberries, strawberries, and blackberries. What a rainbow I have! My berry cobbler is simply easy and ideal for any party, family dinner. It is a classic cobbler recipe that is used by me many years. Let enjoy it together!

Ingredients (13 servings):

baking soda	1 1/2 teaspoons
ground cinnamon	1/2 teaspoon
almond flour	1 1/4 cups
sweetener	3/4 cup
whole milk	1/4 cup
salted butter	2 tablespoons
fresh egg	1 large
fresh raspberries	1 cup
fresh blueberries	1 cup
fresh blackberries	1 cup
fresh strawberries	1 cup
fresh lemon juice	1 tablespoon
kosher salt	1/4 teaspoon

Directions:
1. Take a medium bowl and combine baking soda with cinnamon, almond flour, and ¼ cup sweetener, stir well everything. (Divide flour and sweetener into halves).

2. Whisk together in a small bowl whole milk, melted butter, freshly cracked egg.
3. Add dry ingredients to milk mixture; stir just until moistened and set aside.
4. Wash all the berries thoroughly. Toss the berries in a large bowl, add lemon juice and salt, the remaining amount of sugar and remained almond flour in a medium bowl.
5. Spray the cooking spray over the bottom and sides of the Crock Pot.
6. Transfer the berry mixture to the Crock Pot, cover and cook on LOW for 2-3 hours.
7. Bon Appetite!

Cranberry Upside-Down Cake

What could be easier to cook than the cranberry upside-down cake? Really, I don't know! Everything you need to do here – it is to mix all the ingredients listed below (follow my instructions) and pour the mixture into the Crock Pot. Turn on the mentioned position and wait with patience until the cake is done! Enjoy it right now!

Ingredients (12 servings):

Sweetener	1 cup
butter melted	1/2 cup
whole-berry cranberry sauce	1 (14-oz.) can
fresh cranberries	1 (12-oz.) package

milk	3/4 cup
eggs	2 large
almond extract	1/2 teaspoon
Vanilla ice cream (if desired)	

For cake mix (homemade):

Almond flour	2 3/4 cup
Sweetener	1 3/4 cups
baking soda	2 teaspoon
salt	3/4 teaspoon

Directions:

1. Whisk together all the ingredients for the cake mix using a medium-sized bowl (sweetener, almond flour, salt, baking soda).
2. Take a small bowl and toss the sweetener, melted butter, and sauce. Mix until smooth texture.
3. Spray the Crock Pot with cooking spray and pour the mixture into the Crock Pot. Top with the cranberries.
4. Using the blender or the food processor, mix cake mix (homemade), milk, fresh eggs, almond extract, vanilla until smooth. It takes you usually 1 minute.
5. Pour the batter over cranberries in the Crock Pot. Cover it and cook on HIGH for

1,5-2 hours, check with a toothpick inserted in the center. It must come out clean.
6. Turn off the Crock Pot and let the cake cool for about 25 minutes.
7. Remove the cake to a serving plate.
8. Serve with the ice cream, at will.
9. Bon Appetite!

Cinnamon Bread Pudding Crock Pot

The cinnamon bread pudding is great for supper, dinner, and breakfast! You may eat it even at your lunchtime, it is perfectly well! All the ingredients are easy to find in the stores and they don't cost too much. Try to cook it for your family and friends.

Ingredients (10 servings):

eggs, beaten	3 large
sweetener	1/2 cup
ground cinnamon	1 teaspoon
ground nutmeg	1/4 teaspoon
milk	1 cup
whipping cream	1 cup
vanilla extract	1 teaspoon
butter melted	2 tablespoons

cinnamon keto bread loaf, cut into 1-inch cubes
1 (1-pound)

pecans toasted   1/2 cup

Whipped cream at will

Directions:
1. Take a middle-sized bowl and blend together fresh cracked eggs, sweetener, cinnamon and nutmeg. Chop the pecans.
2. Stir in milk, vanilla, cream and melted butter.
3. Add the cubes of bread, after conjoining the pecans. Stir thoroughly until bread is almost moistened. Cover and roast about an hour.
4. Spray the Crock Pot with the cooking spray, pour the mixture into the Crock Pot; cover with the aluminum foil.
5. Pour a cup of water into the Crock Pot (put a wire rack to fit cooker on the bottom).
6. Cover the lid and cook on LOW 5 hours or until a fork comes out clean.
7. Cool bread before serving.
8. Serve warm with whipped cream, at will.
9. Bon Appetite!

Matcha Crock Pot Souffle

This tasty dessert treats for those who like soufles! The Matcha Crock Pot Souffle is a sweetened whipped dessert with green matcha, fresh raspberries with chocolate and whipping cream.

Ingredients (9 servings):
Eggs   3 large pcs

Swerve confectioners	2 tablespoons
vanilla extract	1 teaspoon
matcha powder	1 tablespoon
butter	1 tablespoon
raspberries	7 whole
coconut oil	1 tablespoon
unsweetened cocoa powder	1 tablespoon
whipped cream	¼ cup

Directions:

1. Separate the eggs into whites and yolks.
2. Whip the egg whites in a bowl of a medium-size with the one tablespoon of Swerve confectioners. Add matcha powder. Continue to whip until smooth consistency.
3. Take another large bowl, using a fork break up the yolks. Mix in the vanilla, after this, add a small amount of the already whipped whites. Fold the rest of the egg whites into the yolk mix.
4. Open the Crock Pot, add the melted butter. Add the souffle mixture to the Crock Pot. Set on LOW for 2 hours and put the raspberries on top.
5. Once the cooking time is over or the top starts to brown, remove the soufflé from the Crock Pot.

6. Melt the coconut oil in a saucepan, whisk in the cocoa powder and the rest Swerve confectioners. Drizzle across the top.
7. Serve with whipped cream.
8. Bon Appetite!

Keto Brownies Crock Pot

Today I decided to cook our lovely brownies flourless in the Crock Pot. I think you love the brownies too... don't waste time and run to the kitchen!

Ingredients (7 servings):

low-carb milk chocolate	5 ounces
butter	4 tablespoons
eggs	3 large pcs
Sweetener	½ cup
mascarpone cheese	¼ cup
unsweetened cocoa powder	¼ cup
salt	½ teaspoon

Directions:
1. Melt the chocolate in a medium-sized saucepan over a medium heat for a little, stirring each time until smooth consistency.
2. Melt the butter and stir everything well. Continue until smooth. Set aside and let it cool.

3. Take a large bowl, beat the eggs and whisk with granulated sweetener on high until the mix becomes frothy and the eggs are pale. It should take about 4-5 minutes.
4. Add the mascarpone cheese to the bowl and beat until smooth.
5. Add the cocoa powder and salt and mix everything well.
6. Sift in the rest of the cocoa powder and stir.
7. Be sure the chocolate is still melted. Pour the melted chocolate into the batter and mix thoroughly until it is creamy.
8. Open the Crock Pot, pour batter and set on HIGH for 2 hours.
9. Remove from the Crock Pot and let it cool completely!
10. Bon Appetite!
1. Serve warm.

Conclusion

Trying something new, for example, new diet, we usually wonder – if the chosen method suitable for me? How can I avoid eating forbidden products? What must I cook today? Is it boring? How many times should I go shopping? It is a total misconception, I think if a person thinks the ketogenic diet is just eating boring food without some variety of recipes and tasty combinations. The recipes of this cookbook contain a huge number of recipes from single portions to full meals that could feed the whole your family and friends, reasoning how easy and tasty could be the keto diet. But what about if you are always in a hurry, busy, have a big family? Maybe you have no mood to cook at all? Is the cooking process boring for you? You don't like washing pile of dishes all the time, don't you? I have gathered all the keto-friendly recipes that you may cook in the Crock Pot! It solves all your problems. No need to spend a lot of time on the stove, no need to search on the Internet for hours trying to follow the keto-rules and keeping in the mind necessary information all the time. I have done all these jobs for you! I think the ketogenic diet is the easiest and simplest way one could choose to burn fat in the body for energy. This cookbook will definitely help you to say «Goodbye» to preferred bread, potatoes, rice and pasta, and to say warm greetings to oils and cheese. The ketogenic diet really works if you follow the rules posted on the food list (forbidden and allowed products) and the genius Crock Pot helps you in the achievement of the aim. Think about your health – Could you do something useful for it right now? Consuming of heart-healthy fats decrease the possible risk of heart diseases, the limitation of sweets and sugar lowers the risk of diabetes type 2. Of course, eating keto-friendly food doesn't mean to consume ice cream or any kind of fat all the time. There is a huge variety of products low in carbohydrates and full of fat that is advised you at the recipes of this keto Crock Pot cookbook.

Do check out my other books that helps you eat healthier, burn fat & to live an active lifestyle!

Keto Diet Crock Pot Cookbook: Healthy, Easy and Fast Keto Recipes, includes a 28-day Ketogenic Diet Plan to get off to a Great Start

Author's Afterthoughts

Thanks ever so much to each of my cherished readers for investing the time read this book!

I know you could have picked from many other books but you chose this one. So big thanks for downloading this book and reading all way to the end.

If you enjoyed this book or received value from it, I'd like to ask you for a favor. Please take a few minutes to post an honest and heartfelt review on Amazon.com Your support does make a difference and to benefit other people.

תודה
Dankie Gracias
Спасибо Merci شكرا Takk
Köszönjük Terima kasih
Grazie Dziękujemy Děkojame
Ďakujeme Vielen Dank Paldies
Kiitos Täname teid 谢谢
Thank You Tak
感謝您 Obrigado Teşekkür Ederiz
감사합니다
Σας ευχαριστούμε ขอบคุณ
Bedankt Děkujeme vám
ありがとうございます
Tack

Made in the USA
San Bernardino, CA
16 March 2019